MEET THE ꓕꓳꓑLE

WHY BUSINESSES MUST ENGAGE WITH PUBLIC OPINION TO MANAGE AND ENHANCE THEIR REPUTATIONS

JAMES FRAYNE

Hh

HARRIMAN HOUSE LTD

3A Penns Road
Petersfield
Hampshire
GU32 2EW
GREAT BRITAIN

Tel: +44 (0)1730 233870
Email: enquiries@harriman-house.com
Website: www.harriman-house.com

First published in Great Britain in 2013

Copyright © Harriman House

The right of James Frayne to be identified as the Author has been asserted in accordance with the Copyright, Design and Patents Act 1988.

ISBN: 9780857192578

British Library Cataloguing in Publication Data
A CIP catalogue record for this book can be obtained from the British Library.

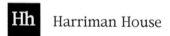 Harriman House

CONTENTS

eBook edition

As a buyer of the print edition of *Meet the People* you can now download the eBook edition free of charge to read on an eBook reader, your smartphone or your computer. Simply go to:

http://ebooks.harriman-house.com/meetthepeople

Or point your smartphone at the QRC.

You can then register and download your free eBook.

Follow us on Twitter – **@harrimanhouse** – for the latest on new titles and special offers.

www.harriman-house.com   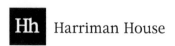 Harriman House

ABOUT THE AUTHOR

JAMES FRAYNE HAS worked at the highest levels of corporate, political, and government communications. He was Director of Communications for a British government department between 2011 and 2012, having previously worked for some of the biggest brands in the world in communications agencies in London and for a number of high-profile political campaigns.

James began his career working for Business for Sterling, the successful campaign against British membership of the European single currency, and he managed the No campaign against the proposed North East Regional Assembly in the 2004 referendum, which won an upset landslide against the government-backed Yes campaign.

He also worked for the think tank Reform – helping launch the Doctors for Reform campaign to change the NHS – and has been campaign director of the TaxPayers' Alliance. In 2011 the political editor of the *Guardian* described him as being "one of the best Tory-leaning media strategists".

As a campaign spokesman and analyst, James has appeared widely in broadcast media, including BBC One's *Breakfast News*, the BBC News Channel, Sky News, Radio 4's *Today Programme* and *PM Programme*, BBC Radio 5 Live, and on numerous local BBC TV and radio stations and international TV stations.

He has written for *The Spectator, Daily Telegraph, City A.M.*, the BBC News website, *The Business* magazine, *PR Week, CorpComms* magazine, and various blogs, including Conservative Home. The editor of Conservative Home named James' blog – Campaign War Room – Blog of the Year in 2010.

ACKNOWLEDGEMENTS

THIS BOOK WAS only possible because of the career I have enjoyed so far in communications and that was dependent on help and inspiration I received from friends and colleagues along the way. Some people deserve a particular mention.

Dominic Cummings, now a government adviser, combines a razor sharp intellect with exceptional operational ability, and introduced me to many of the ideas in this book. Nick Herbert MP and George Eustice MP were superb early bosses in the campaign world and Michael Gove MP showed me up close how politicians operate at the highest levels consistently. James Bethell of Westbourne and Tim Allan of Portland brought me into the corporate communications world and provided extremely useful guidance and support. Terry Nelson of FP1 Strategies and Republican consultant Chris LaCivita have provided inspiration from across the pond.

I received a great deal of help in the production of this book. Dr Jamie MacIntosh of the University College London-based Institute for Security & Resilience Studies and Professor Alison Wolf of King's College London provided insightful comments on drafts, as did Piotr Brzezinski. A number of top consultants in the UK and elsewhere were also kind enough to explain their views and approach to issues raised in this book. Myles Hunt and Craig Pearce of Harriman House have been very encouraging and helpful throughout this process.

Finally, I owe more than I can say to my brilliant wife Rachel Wolf – on this project and on everything else – and this book is for her.

AUTHOR'S NOTE

I HAVE BEEN working in the worlds of business, politics and government for 15 years, often dealing with confidential and sensitive information. Furthermore, many of the issues I worked on are still live and colleagues are still in place.

For these reasons, I have only explicitly referenced past campaigns and projects where they are officially over, or where my work or my organisation's work are already in the public domain. I have been necessarily obscure or vague about some other work.

The chances are that readers are working in the world of communications themselves and will no doubt understand this and forgive me for it. My first responsibility is to my current and past clients and colleagues.

INTRODUCTION
MEET THE PEOPLE

THE EXPLOSION OF PUBLIC OPINION

THIS IS A book about *people*. Like it or not, a revolution has taken place in communications and democracy has finally arrived. Ordinary people now determine what the world thinks about even the biggest businesses.

The explosive growth of the web, and above all social media, means every minute of the day across the world, people share opinions on what they have bought, the actions of businesses in the public eye, and what they think about issues that concern modern firms, such as taxes and regulation. Out of nowhere, these opinions are dragging businesses into major public conversations that trample on their carefully-constructed brand images.

Sites like Facebook (**www.facebook.com**) and Twitter (**www.twitter.com**) are the tip of the iceberg – there is a panoply of other social media channels. Sites like Amazon (**www.amazon.co.uk**) allow people to rate and review an array of consumer goods, Goodreads (**www.goodreads.com**) allows people to rate old and new books, and TripAdvisor (**www.tripadvisor.com**) does the same for hotels, restaurants and tourist attractions.

In the UK, Mumsnet (**www.mumsnet.com**) gives mothers the chance to discuss products and services for their children, Auto Trader (**www.autotrader.co.uk**) provides a platform for customer reviews of cars and Beer in the Evening (**www.beerintheevening.com**) is a site where people rate pubs and bars. Specialist site Money Saving Expert (**www.moneysavingexpert.com**) provides advice on personal finance, while Honest John (**www.honestjohn.co.uk**) gives guidance on used cars; both encourage public discussion.

In the US, Angie's List (**www.angieslist.com**) acts as a clearing house for reviews on businesses providing local services, people discuss their lecturers at Rate My Professors (**blog.ratemyprofessors.com**) and Cinemascore (**www.cinemascore.com**) provides data on the public's reaction to film releases that were previously only available to major studios. These sites – and many others – are replacing the established media as the first place people turn to for guidance on where to go and what to buy.

The public now has mass publishing power on an extraordinary scale. Fifteen years ago, when the web started to take off meaningfully, the online world was dominated by early adopters and existing elites. People went on the web to read the news, to view information, and buy goods and services. Now they increasingly use the web to *talk*.

The growth of visible public opinion online is important for the corporate world for three reasons. Firstly, the scale of these online, public conversations is huge. Major public-facing businesses are being discussed constantly by enormous numbers of people. Anyone with a passing interest in a business will come across strong opinions on that business regularly. Those that take the time to do a specific search for views on a business or its sector will be left in no doubt about what people think.

Secondly, the conversations taking place on some businesses are the *only* conversations taking place about them. After all, most firms do not appear daily or even weekly in the mainstream media and most do not run constant, major advertising campaigns. The only influential views on some businesses people may see come from these conversations.

Thirdly – and it is crucial businesses accept this point – contrary to what some in the media believe, people take the views of other people they know, or that appear to be similar to them, seriously. On many issues, people actually *prefer* to hear the views of ordinary consumers rather than those of the established commentators the media themselves believe are insightful.

The democratic forces shaping the image of the corporate world are turning reputation management upside down. Public opinion has not only replaced news as being the most important external force in shaping the ongoing image and reputation of a business, but its power is now so strong that it more than rivals business' own marketing and advertising campaigns in determining how they are perceived.

THE END OF ELITE COMMUNICATIONS

Until very recently, an airline that wanted to shape its reputation might show journalists a fine time in the hope of a positive write up that stressed how good the food was and how nice the staff were. Now, that same airline is dealing with people complaining on Twitter about the nightmare of checking in, that their bags got lost, and that their rivals are better. Dealing with the latter challenge demands a completely different way of operating.

It is hard to overstate the significance of this change. Since its inception in a recognisable form in the 1920s, corporate communications has been a top-down, elite affair. Powerful elites not only owned the platforms of communications – newspapers, radio stations, cinema studios, publishing houses, and, later, TV studios – they generated the content they also marketed. This was a constant period of elite transmission – with the public expected to sit and read, watch, or listen to material created for them.

Writing in *Propaganda*, the classic work of 1928, Edward Bernays, known as the *father of public relations*, was clear about the potential modern mass communications offered:

"The minority has discovered a powerful help in influencing majorities... It has been found possible so to mold the mind of the masses that they will throw their newly gained strength in the desired direction... Whatever of social importance is done today, whether in politics, finance, manufacture, agriculture, charity, education, or other fields, must be done with the help of propaganda. Propaganda is the executive arm of the invisible Government."[1]

Bernays' was the prevalent view in the decades that followed. Read the seminal works of the post-war corporate communications world – books like David Ogilvy's *Confessions of an Advertising Man* (1963), Tony Schwartz's *The Responsive Chord* (1974), or Lester Wunderman's *Being Direct* (1996) – and, brilliant as they are, you will see few references to the public being a competing force in shaping corporate reputation.

In this old world, businesses could reasonably expect the scale of their advertising and marketing to create the image they designed, while competent media relations would protect it. The views of the general public were almost completely hidden. Businesses have always been aware of the ultimate public judgements on their operations through sales figures, but unless they commissioned ongoing opinion research they would have no real sense of what the public thought about them day-to-day.

That is not to say the corporate communications world necessarily looked down on the public, but instead that the views of the public on businesses were irrelevant. No up-and-coming consultant would look to secure favourable comments from their boss by raising questions about what the views of a business' brand might be in provincial England.

This elite stranglehold over the communications industry began to break down in the 1990s. The growth of competing news outlets (like BSkyB in Britain, for example) was undoubtedly a factor in fracturing the dominance of traditional elites. .

But the real growth in public power came with the development of the web, and above all social media. Since the latter years of the first decade of this century, all of the old assumptions around corporate communications have been swept away.

AN OPINION ISSUE, NOT A WEB ISSUE

What is it that businesses are dealing with here?

In my experience, too many businesses view the explosion of opinion online as being a simple *web issue*. They look at what is being said about them on Facebook, Twitter, YouTube, and the web generally, and instinctively look first to improve their own capabilities on these platforms.

But businesses do not have a simple web issue; they have a *public opinion* issue that manifests itself primarily online. While it would be an exaggeration to say businesses should disregard the fact public conversation happens to take place on the web, they should be thinking *people* first, *technology* second.

This might seem an obvious point, but businesses have to remember that while the culture of the web and social media encourages a certain style and tone from those that engage online, sites like Twitter and Facebook are merely platforms for people to air their opinions – platforms that are not only extremely quick and convenient to use but which almost guarantee people will be heard. The opinions that people make known are exactly the same as those they express to family members at home or their friends on a night out; the web is merely the vehicle.

A business that became skilled on Facebook might make its site look attractive using pictures and video, and find ways of monitoring commentary effectively and updating their page remotely. However, if the general content is weak and the arguments used unpersuasive, this expertise will be wasted.

Above all, businesses need to become experts in public opinion. They must understand what moves people and how different types of people are affected by public debate. They need to understand what affects people's opinions on their business specifically and their area of operation. And they need to remember they are not interacting with rational machines, but with people who are probably sitting on their sofas in a small town somewhere in the middle of the country.

WHY POLITICS PROVIDES THE ANSWERS

In this book, I argue businesses must look to political campaigns for lessons on how to meet the challenges of this new democratic world. As I will explain, great campaigns are expert in shifting public opinion – the fundamental challenge that businesses now face. We are used to hearing that politicians must learn from corporate leaders. In this case, the opposite is true.

Using my own experience working at the top of British politics, together with case studies of past campaigns and interviews with some of the best political consultants in Britain and the United States, I reveal the fundamental skills consultants really focus on when they put together high-profile campaigns.

A huge amount has been written over the last few decades about political campaigns. Of this, much has been behind-the-scenes accounts of famous political battles. Interesting and insightful as many of these accounts have been, the lessons for those interested in replicating the success have been at best implied. Of the minority of books that have looked at campaigning as an art, most have covered campaigning skills quite briefly.

I have gone into detail on the fundamental skills that enable campaigns to move public opinion. These are a mix of pure communications skills designed to affect what people think and do, and operational skills that enable campaigns to reach the public in the first place.

Campaigns are, after all, about action – success depends, in part, on being heard.

ABOUT THIS BOOK

HOW THIS BOOK IS STRUCTURED

In chapters one and two I explain how communications has changed, and why lessons from political campaigns will enable businesses to navigate the new world of emotional, often aggressive, public opinion.

In chapters three through seven I describe the fundamentals of successful campaigns, and how businesses can apply them. Those fundamentals are:

1. The scientific approach to developing and disseminating messages.

2. How cognitive and social sciences have taught us how to make messages appeal on an emotional level.

3. Why endorsements and third parties matter.

4. The importance of strategy.

5. Decision-taking and organisational design.

Chapters eight, nine and ten look at how businesses can turn an understanding of these key principles of campaigning into effective action in the real world, so as to shape their reputations. They look at how businesses should shape their reputations online and in the changing media, as well how to manage regular crises.

In the conclusion I explain what this all means in practice for businesses and how they should reform their communications operations to deal with the challenges they face.

Finally, in the appendix, I set out a sketch curriculum for an Advanced Course in Communications. One of the contentions in this book is that the communications industry as a whole – and this includes political campaigns as well as those that operate in the corporate world – does not take learning and development sufficiently seriously and largely leaves staff to learn on the job. The growth of the web and social media – and the exposure to the public this brings – demands a more serious approach to communications.

THE PURPOSE OF THIS BOOK

Books that highlight challenges thrown up by change can emphasise threats everywhere at the expense of opportunities. This is not my intention. I happen to believe the growth of the web and the greater role for the public in shaping the reputation of businesses is a good thing.

In my career, I have successfully helped many businesses exploit the opportunities created by the explosion of opinion and their exposure to it. I have helped businesses completely redefine issues surrounding their activities by mobilising ordinary people on their behalf and showing the outside world the public is on their side. There is a strong opportunity for the corporate world here, because businesses that elites in government and the media could once ignore or demonise now have the tools to more than fight back. The web gives them the ability to recruit and mobilise public supporters behind their corporate goals.

But it would be naïve to pretend every business welcomes the changes that have come about as a result of the web and social media. In my experience, they do not. Businesses like to stay in control and minimise surprises; direct exposure to public opinion, even where it offers theoretical opportunities, worries them. For these reasons, I spend time dwelling on the challenges businesses face in this new world, but focus overall on the principles of how businesses should seek to affect public opinion in their favour.

This is not intended to be a simple *how-to* guide on dealing with challenges from social media. While I give specific suggestions for action online and elsewhere in latter chapters, the bulk of this book focuses on campaign fundamentals. This is because, the more organisations I work with in this new world where public opinion is *all*, the more I believe it is these fundamentals that really matter. Frankly, I believe anyone can learn the specific tactical skills required to navigate the web relatively easily, while the art of public persuasion is another matter entirely.

Some of the principles explained in this book – and therefore the implied lessons – are very simple. That does not make them easy. People that think developing and applying an approach that focuses on public opinion requires minimal change – or that these skills are widespread in corporate communications – are mistaken. Anyone taking a meaningful look at the way most corporate communications teams are structured and the way they engage with the public will see that they are failing to cope with the fresh challenges arising in this new world.

Those businesses that act upon the lessons in this book will have a radically different – and much more successful – approach than those who do not.

CHAPTER ONE
THE RISE OF PEOPLE POWER

HOW THE WEB CHANGED COMMUNICATIONS

IN JANUARY 2013 Matt Corby, an Australian customer of sandwich chain SUBWAY, bought a classic "footlong" sandwich. Suspicious, he decided to measure it. After discovering the sandwich was only eleven inches in length Corby posted the photographic evidence on Facebook. SUBWAY was catapulted into a major brand crisis.

Initially, SUBWAY stood its ground, reasonably arguing "footlong" was a brand name rather than a description of length. It did not work and the issue continued to gather attention and momentum. The *New York Post* sent people out to buy seven footlong sandwiches and four came in undersized.[2] Inevitably, perhaps, two disgruntled customers threatened legal action because of SUBWAY's alleged deception. The restaurant finally managed to close the story down when they stripped away all the nuance, expressed regret and gave a firm commitment to meet the footlong standard across the world.[3]

The crisis developed with a single customer's negative opinion. His Facebook post was passed on and snowballed until the mainstream media picked it up. Within days SUBWAY had a serious problem on their hands. Ten years ago, the worst case scenario would have been an angry letter from Mr Corby appearing in a small Australian newspaper.

In February 2013, Bill Samuels Jr., the son of the founder of Maker's Mark, announced the firm was going to water down its bourbon to meet a worldwide increase in demand. (Drinks like bourbon cannot just be made to order in the short term – bourbon has to mature.) Samuels announced Maker's Mark was going to reduce the alcohol by volume from 45% to 42%, to make supplies go further. The business assured customers they would not notice the difference.

The response on social media – particularly on Maker's Mark's own Facebook page – was extremely negative. Accusations poured in – the business was no longer committed to quality and did not care about its customers. Within days the leadership decided to reverse their decision, apologising to customers.

What would have happened 15, or even ten, years ago? Some Maker's Mark enthusiasts may have written to the firm to express opposition, but the need to write a letter or pick up the phone means fewer people would have registered their concerns – and those concerns would have taken weeks to filter through.

Even more importantly, only the firm would have seen the complaints. Social media made commenting quick and easy, and made it *public*. That encouraged other, less fanatical, customers to pitch in. Opposition noise came louder and faster than it otherwise would have done and the firm probably had no real option but to back down.[4]

In 2012, when New York Mayor Michael Bloomberg supported a ban on certain sugar-sweetened drinks over 16 ounces, the immediate reaction of many in the soft drinks trade was to form an online campaign to recruit corporate and public support and to shape opinion in their favour. This included a website giving people information about the issue, a Twitter stream and a Facebook page to publicise their case.

By the middle of 2013, with a legal battle over the status of the ban underway, New Yorkers for Beverage Choices claimed over half a million supporters and over 3,700 coalition members. While the campaign has had a presence in the mainstream media, which is clearly still significant in a city like New York where newspapers and TV really matter, the campaign was able to demonstrate greater visibility and authenticity by publicly mobilising businesses and people online.

THE PUBLIC CONVERSATION ON MODERN BUSINESSES

The stories I include above are just three examples of wider trends taking place in corporate communications. All day, every day, ordinary people take to the web to air their opinions on modern businesses and the issues that affect them – and to share those opinions with the rest of the world. These conversations are so large in scale they are coming to dominate the public's view of businesses.

At the time of writing it is spring 2013 and I type "Shell Oil" into Twitter. I see the following: comments from non-governmental organisations (NGOs) about Shell's decision not to drill in the Arctic; unclear but negative comments relating to their tax affairs; references to the Iraq War being about oil; and the odd comment pointing to mainstream media coverage about the company. Those comments are collectively visible to millions.

I type in "British Airways" and see the following: a positive comment about the quality of BA's food; criticism over delays; a few references to apparently missing baggage; some positive comments about BA's interaction on Twitter; and some non-specific negative comments about their customer service. It is a mixed bag, with a number of positive comments mixed in with criticism. BA's own Twitter feed engages with people directly and is polite, lively and helpful.

Next, to Facebook. Here I find a number of groups hostile to Shell. There are a number of groups against their fracking operations, the size of these ranging from a small number of supporters to many hundreds. British Airways generally comes out well on Facebook. Its own Facebook page is attractive and engaging, and people take a positive approach to the airline. There are other Facebook pages that criticise them – one criticises their cabin crew while another criticises them over strikes – although these have small numbers of followers.

Shell and British Airways were chosen at random. They are in very different businesses with their own challenges and the extent of their exposure to consumers also differs. Shell has an extensive network of petrol stations while BA exists purely to serve its vast number of customers. But, despite their differences, both still find themselves being defined by the public.

Similar searches on restaurant chains, banks, transport firms, healthcare providers, hotel chains, travel firms and operators in a wide variety of other sectors reveal businesses being discussed by the public in similar ways. Some businesses are more exposed than others, but an ever-increasing number of firms are talked about regardless of their formal links to consumers.

It is the public – ordinary people from every walk of life – taking part in these conversations. While some conversations are instigated by NGOs and campaigns, they do not account for the bulk of public commentary. As in everyday life, some people have particularly loud or dominant voices in debate, but the type of people involved as participants is wide-ranging.

For many businesses, the challenges arising from the growth of the web are intensified by specific public-facing websites that deal with their area of operation. Businesses that work in the hospitality sector find their products and services discussed in extreme detail on sites like TripAdvisor or Yelp. While they used to rely on a favourable review in a mainstream media outlet, they now find themselves reviewed weekly or daily by demanding members of the public and then ranked based upon their ratings. A restaurant can no longer rely on a decades-long reputation. It has to be good today – or its customers pass public judgement.

Contrast this with how these businesses are reported in the mainstream media – where respect and objectivity are virtually guaranteed. Journalists almost always provide context, even for difficult stories, and the statements businesses provide are given reasonable prominence within the story. Again, while some businesses do better than others, there is usually an attempt by the media to be reasonable and balanced.

THE POWER OF THE PUBLIC VOICE

We have become used to a world where the web and social media are integral parts of people's daily lives. The fact that ordinary people are taking to Twitter and Facebook and making their opinions heard is no surprise to us. It is amazing how quickly we all become emotionally accustomed to change, getting used to revolution as being the new reality very quickly. But this familiarity should not blind us to the extraordinary change this has on the worlds of reputation management and corporate communications.

The world of corporate communications has been completely changed. In just a few years, we have moved from a position where the public voice was completely unheard, to one where it is now crucial in shaping what the world thinks about businesses. Businesses that have worked for decades under the assumption that advertising and marketing set their image – and media relations and public affairs shaped it – are finding that ordinary people across the world are becoming increasingly important.

The scale of the conversation online is extraordinary and it continues to grow at pace. According to the most recent figures available from UK telecoms regulator Ofcom, three-quarters of British people have broadband internet, half of all British adults use social networking sites at home, and around 40% of people use their mobile phones to access the internet.[5]

In the United States, Pew Research found that 85% of Americans use the internet[6] and 67% of internet users access social media sites.[7] Pew also found that 78% of internet users look for online information about a product or service (2010 data) and 37% would themselves rate a product or service using an online rating system (2011 data).[8]

It is clear the actual and potential audiences for all of this opinion are massive and the numbers of people who will actively post their own opinions regularly are extremely significant. The scale of the public conversations around businesses is therefore vast and this cannot but have a major effect on their reputation. While specific websites and social media platforms may come and go, the interaction that comes from the web is now embedded within people's daily lives and this trend towards public commentary on businesses will intensify.

It is important to understand the difference between those that contribute actively to the online conversation and those that watch it. For many, the web is about watching and learning rather than taking part. Businesses must therefore not take false comfort from seeing only small numbers of negative statements about them online or get depressed about the small number of positive comments. They need to remember the numbers of people who will actually see those comments and have their view affected.

It can be tempting for some to think of personal opinions that appear online as being less relevant or credible than those that appear in the mainstream media. After all, many of the opinions aired are eccentric in the extreme or visibly very one-sided and many are made by people with only small numbers of followers.

The reality is, regardless of what some executives might hope, these opinions emphatically do matter. While a single tweet from one person to their 50 followers is insignificant, very significant numbers of people tweeting to their 50 followers is a different matter – with social media, the cumulative effect of public activity is important. A series of tweets from people with small numbers of followers with an amusing or interesting hashtag can see an issue or a business trend on Twitter within an hour, dragging far more people into the conversation.

Also, while some opinions lack credibility, it is wrong to assume the opinions of ordinary people are taken less seriously than those of established journalists. A 2012 survey of global internet users by consumer research specialists Nielsen showed that 70% trust consumer opinions posted online, compared to 58% that trust editorial content such as newspaper articles. Ads on TV and in magazines were trusted by less than half.[9] People trust other people like them, and those not seen as self-interested or biased.

OPINION IN THE MAINSTREAM MEDIA

The explosion of opinion on the web, posted there by ordinary people, is game changing for modern businesses. This has been exacerbated by simultaneous changes in the media, which is becoming increasingly opinionated. These changes are occurring in three ways: online news stories now often resemble blogs; reporters themselves are becoming players in the world they used simply to report on; and a very obvious feedback loop now operates between ordinary people and the media via social media and the web.

Newspapers are massively expanding the amount of copy they are putting online and their websites are updated multiple times a day. Many of these stories will never make it to the hard copy of the newspaper and were never intended to. These stories are often lighter on facts, and heavier on opinion, even if that opinion is mostly *implied* opinion from the direction of the story.

For example, a classic online story now is the *sparked fury* story; it seems to be written multiple times a day. In it, a journalist will pick up on a vaguely controversial comment by a politician, senior corporate executive or celebrity and then call around individuals or groups who can give a representative response quote to generate a row. The reporter can then write up a few hundred words on how the well-known person's comments "sparked fury", and then hopefully a few hundred more if the well-known person clarifies their views.

Often, well-known people *will* say remarkable things that should and do spark fury, but often journalists seem to manufacture rows on the most trivial of issues. These are not objective reports but amount to opinionated blog pieces. At the same time, a large number of news reporters, including those at respected outlets, have used their own Twitter feeds and blogs to air their personal opinions on developing stories.

While such Twitter feeds usually have the disclaimer "Tweets are made in a personal capacity," this is a complete irrelevance. The journalists are not read because of their innate wisdom, but because they work for well-known publications. Their tweeting clearly blurs the line between objective news and personal opinion, particularly when reporters tweet views on a story online, while narrating it *factually* in print. Some journalists increasingly find themselves in the questionable position of being players in a game they should be objectively reporting on.

Finally, stories increasingly pick up on opinions and comments aired online by ordinary people – turning them into news simply by writing about them. There are regularly news stories on issues like chaos at airports and train stations, almost exclusively based on comments picked up from social media platforms. Twitter comments are regularly fed into news stories online that provide instant reaction to events.

Social media and the mainstream media now operate in a constant feedback loop. In a newsworthy time like a major international product launch, the media will pick up on comments by ordinary people on the product and put them in their stories. More ordinary people see these stories and add their own opinions to them, creating a feedback loop with the potential to cause serious reputational damage to businesses.

The mainstream media is on a journey from news to opinion. New online entrants are joining the established media scene and consciously blur the lines between news and comment – for example, Politico and the Daily Beast. As newspaper budgets shrink, forcing some to close or go online completely, cheap and fast comment will start replacing news that is time-consuming and expensive to generate and report. Opinion will become ever more dominant.

WHAT THE EXPLOSION OF OPINION MEANS IN PRACTICE

The growth of the web and social media is rapidly changing the way corporate communications teams operate. Jon Steinberg, former deputy director of communications for Democrat Senate Majority Leader Harry Reid and part of John Kerry's 2004 Presidential campaign, now works as a senior corporate communications consultant. He told me he sees three obvious changes from the growth of the web and social media for businesses:

> "First, it's changed where stories come from. For a consumer business, the ability of a Twitter user to initiate a round of stories or a Facebook protest to create negative headlines means that the communications team has much less control over the news flow on their brands.

> "Second, it has created new channels for communicating directly to consumers without the filter of the media. A kind of third way between paid and earned media means that brands are able to get messages directly to their consumers and through data analytics, understand much better than ever before what messages will be most effective in driving consumer behaviour. Businesses can communicate without ever dealing with the media.

> "Finally, it has accelerated the news cycle to being perpetual. A story can develop from anywhere at anytime. Media handlers have to be equally adept at spotting stories, responding to inquiries and pushing out narratives. At the same time, brands also have to be a bit more thick skinned in understanding that in the social media space, there is less control over brand perception and anyone can be a critic. Developing the judgment to understand what must be responded to and what should be left to lie low is as, if not more, important than writing a snappy sound bite."[10]

Mark Wallace was previously head of media relations at the Institute of Directors, which represents tens of thousands of British businesses, and is now executive editor of the Conservative Home website, one of the most important UK political sites. He agrees the changes have been immense:

> "The growth of digital and social media has utterly changed the game for corporate communicators. On every issue, public involvement is now faster, more direct, more intense and better informed.

> "This is a liberating experience for communicators, because the power of middle-men in traditional media has been diluted, providing a huge opportunity to speak to audiences directly. But it also ramps up the risks involved – negative news is now guaranteed to get out, and reaction to it can become a firestorm in the space of minutes. The good news is that the old approach of spin, command and control PR and nepotism is dead and buried. The bad news is that PR is now more like juggling cigarette lighters in a fireworks factory. It requires a fundamental change in approach, mentality and skills."[11]

The explosion of opinion online has therefore undoubtedly made life more difficult on a day-to-day basis for corporate communications professionals. It has increased uncertainty and exposed them more regularly to real chaos. However, more insightful professionals recognise that the web opens up new opportunities for businesses to define themselves positively by speaking directly to the public and mobilising them.

The challenge for businesses is therefore in trying to manage uncertainty as far as possible and trying to exploit these new opportunities. They should be looking to political campaigns for inspiration on how best to achieve this.

CHAPTER TWO
HOW BUSINESS RESEMBLES POLITICS

THE NEW SIMILARITIES BETWEEN BUSINESS AND POLITICS

THE WORLDS OF corporate and political communications have always been linked. Political consultants from government, campaigns and think tanks have often moved into corporate communications and back again. Businesses value the experience that political consultants bring – particularly their media relationships and their experience advising senior people in difficult circumstances. Despite this, political campaigns and corporate communications have traditionally been totally different in structure, delivery and priorities.

The massive changes that we have seen in corporate communications in the last five years – with the direct exposure to the public as a result of the growth of the web and social media – means corporate communications increasingly resembles political campaigning. In communications terms, both are now engaged in a constant battle to shape attitudes towards their organisations in public conversation.

There are three main ways corporate communications increasingly resembles politics:

1. Exposure to emotional and aggressive criticism.

2. Exposure to scrutiny.

3. Operating in an uncertain and fast-paced environment.

In the remainder of this chapter, I explain these three areas in more detail before going on to explain what businesses can learn from political campaigns as they prepare their response.

1. AGGRESSIVE AND EMOTIONAL DEBATE

Political campaigns have always had extensive exposure to the public. Public opinion on candidates and their campaigns has always been visible through the following channels: the vast number of polls appearing in newspapers; town hall meetings; constituency meetings; the comments from voters when campaigns knock on doors and deliver leaflets; vox pops on TV; the letters pages of the newspapers; and more.

Campaigns are accustomed to emotional and frequently hostile opinion and commentary. They are accustomed to having their senior leaders' past records attacked, the ethics of their donations criticised, and their personal relationships questioned. They deal with these issues every day. Social media has intensified and sped up, but not fundamentally changed, that environment.

Businesses, however, have been shielded from public opinion in the past. But, as we saw in the last chapter, businesses are now being criticised in brutal terms all the time – and directly by members of the public. They are criticised for the quality and cost of their products, their customer service, their ethics and corporate practices, and their senior leaders' pay.

Employers and owners of businesses are being harshly and publicly criticised, in ways not dissimilar to politicians. This is a huge culture shock for many in business. I have worked with dozens of CEOs and senior executives facing personal criticism on the web and on social media platforms. Coming from politics, I was often surprised at people's reaction to such criticism. Even very senior executives hate this sort of personal criticism.

Most people in the corporate world are used to treating people with respect and being treated with respect in return. Most of them express themselves in diplomatic ways and did not get into business to be well known or to exercise power. It is therefore surprising and hurtful to them when they face public hostility. Unfortunately, they are going to have to get used to it.

2. INCREASED LEVELS OF SCRUTINY

As well as being more aggressive about businesses, the rise of opinion means people notice more to be aggressive about. Scrutiny has increased.

In national politics, the level of scrutiny is intense. It comes from political opponents using research teams to cast doubt on a campaign. It comes from third parties, such as independent campaign groups. It comes from parliamentary bodies, regulators and quangos that keep a close eye on what happens in the political world. And it comes from the media, particularly in the UK where the national press is strong and aggressive, and where a lack of political advertising on TV means the press knows they have the ability to define a candidate or campaign.

The growth of the web has intensified scrutiny further on political campaigns. But, as with campaigns' exposure to the public, it has not changed it beyond recognition. Candidates and campaigns have always lived with harsh scrutiny. Now there just happens to be a bit more of it.

For businesses the change is more dramatic. There has been some scrutiny in the past from the financial media, particularly around results time and surrounding product launches. A small number of companies have had to deal with hostile NGOs and consumer groups, and their trade press have been influential.

However, the web and social media has massively increased levels of scrutiny. The web has allowed increasing amounts of information – information that used only to be interesting to industry specialists – to be visible to the public. Annual reports, details on costs and profits, and the speeches of senior executives are now visible. Through relatively simple searches, interested parties can also learn a lot about the individuals that run big companies.

Transparency changes things for all businesses, but particularly those with a high public profile or that operate in more controversial fields. For those businesses, nearly all their public communications get scrutinised and commented on. Furthermore, many face major online campaigns organised by hostile NGOs. The pay and benefits of senior staff will be publicly commented on because people now know what these figures are.

3. STORIES BLOWING UP AT HIGH SPEED

In politics, the growth of the web changed the rhythm of campaign life. Stories come out of nowhere in a way that had not been seen even as 24-hour TV news developed. Now, candidates can be asked instantly for a reaction about an event that happened minutes before on the other side of the world. Political campaigns have always been accustomed to a fast pace, but the web takes this to a new level. Campaign staffers have quickly developed expertise to deal with this change.

The change for the corporate world is again greater. The arrival of stories out of a clear blue sky was not unknown in corporate communications – particularly in sectors like energy and transport – but it was unusual. Now difficult stories can come with no notice and on very serious issues. When SUBWAY were discussing the risks that were likely to affect their operations in the coming year, it seems unlikely that anyone would have raised the prospect of a story like the "footlong" controversy. But it happened.

The ease with which people can share ideas and generate simple campaigns online exposes businesses to reputational risks previously only felt by political campaigns. Now, if a senior executive at a well-known firm makes a statement offensive to a particular group of people, online campaigns can spring up instantly denouncing their comments and mobilising people to boycott the business.

We saw this during the latter stages of the US Presidential campaign in 2012, when the restaurant chain Chick-fil-A was dragged into a row about gay marriage. This began with Chick-fil-A's president, Dan Cathy, telling the *Baptist Press* that the business supported the biblical definition of marriage. His comments led to an online backlash from supporters of gay marriage who called for a boycott. This in turn was met with conservatives calling for an "appreciation day".[12]

Political campaigns are used to these sorts of campaigns – people sending in pre-written postcards, or making calls to offices – but this is completely new for most businesses.

★★★

In summary, in the past, while some of the most famous and biggest firms in the world could expect to operate under an intense public spotlight, most did not. Political campaigns, however, always have. They are used to intense scrutiny and emotional and hostile reactions from the media and public, and they know that when crises come, they come quickly. The explosion of opinion is such that corporate reputation management is now very similar to political campaigning.

CAMPAIGN SKILLS THAT MATTER
IN SEARCH OF LESSONS FROM POLITICAL CAMPAIGNS

As political and corporate communications have come to resemble one another much more closely, businesses need to look hard at the campaign world for inspiration on how to respond. The skills that campaigns deploy in leading public conversations are now directly relevant to them.

Unfortunately, businesses will look to much of political commentary in vain for help. The skills that define the best political campaigns are not the skills that many in the media and the outside world assume them to be. Typically, when they retrospectively explain the success of a particular campaign, commentators focus on those things that are new, most visible, and that have most impact on their own lives as reporters and analysts.

For example, after Labour's 1997 landslide victory over the Conservatives, many obsessed about their rapid rebuttal operation. This saw the Labour Party use the rapid deployment of relevant facts, arguments and comment to the media to frame developing arguments in their favour early and to dominate the news cycle. After Barack Obama defeated Senator John McCain in the 2008 US Presidential election, having won a hard fight with Hillary Clinton in the primaries, many focused on his brilliant web campaign that mobilised supporters across the country.

In both cases, excellence in these areas *was* important and should not be ignored. But, while focusing on these issues makes for good copy, the demonstration of tactical skills in these areas was the result of other, more fundamental, competencies. Labour's rebuttal operation or Barack Obama's web campaign could only be developed in the first place and then gain traction because they managed to create the right operating climate.

A campaign that starts off by asking how to create a great web campaign, rebuttal operation, or set of ads will never get going and competent consultants would never begin constructing a campaign with these questions.

Campaigns know that all that matters is affecting how people think and behave. Everything else is secondary. They therefore keep asking what the prerequisites are for effective action in this area. In doing so, they peel back the layers of complexity to focus on the most fundamental skills that enable them to affect public opinion.

Some of these are what you might call *pure* communications skills – skills in the art of influence and persuasion, for example. But others are in the area of campaign mechanics, like organisational design. They know that changing attitudes depends on their ability to get their message out as well as on the quality of the message. A campaign can have the best and most persuasive materials ever produced, but if the mechanics are not in place to make sure people see them, they will be for nothing.

FIVE FACTORS THAT DETERMINE SUCCESS IN INFLUENCING THE PUBLIC

In my experience, there are five really big things that determine success in influencing the public – I will explore these in detail in coming chapters. The first is an obsession with a more scientific approach to communications through testing and targeting. The aim is to work out which arguments are likely to play best with different sections of the voting public and therefore to work out the overall messages of the campaign and where resources should be targeted. As far as possible, the best campaigns seek to minimise uncertainty and guesswork wherever they can, using a more scientific approach to guide their work.

The second big thing is campaigns' skills in creating messages that actually *move* people – which persuade them to think differently about a candidate or a set of issues. Essentially, these skills are in influence and persuasion. While opinion research is a vital part of this process, campaigns focus on the use of emotion, visual messaging and moral authority to appeal to people's hearts. Advances in brain research and social psychology are giving campaigns greater expertise in this area.

The third thing is campaigns' focus on mobilising third parties to change the balance of power within a debate. Campaigns recognise that, regardless of the popularity of their party or their candidate, there are always limits to what obviously self-interested people can say about their own policies or their own qualities. Recruiting and mobilising third parties on their behalf means campaigns can appeal to new groups of people, help make a particular point more powerfully, or emphasise the qualities of a candidate in a way that cannot be done alone. Third parties can inject moral authority into a campaign that cannot be self-generated.

Fourth, campaigns understand that the structure of the organisation matters. You can have the best and most experienced staff available and a great candidate, but campaigns are about action, and that means being able to process vast amounts of information effectively and to take the right decisions quickly and consistently.

For these reasons, campaigns worry endlessly about their decision-taking capability. Related to this, because of the breadth and scale of the challenges they face, campaigns also ensure that their communications operations are as integrated as possible. Media relations, marketing and advertising, social media, and speeches, all sit under the same management so that target audiences are hearing the same consistent message. *Silo-isation* is avoided at all costs.

The fifth and final thing is that campaigns understand the real meaning of strategy and take it seriously. They recognise strategy is not simply about long-term planning – which is a product of strategy – but that it is about providing an *approach* to the operation to overcome challenges and exploit opportunities. Campaigns therefore know what the focus of their operations needs to be and how this relates to their objectives.

★★★

Not every campaign is effective; anyone that follows the political news media will know that some are prone to endless missteps. However, many campaigns exhibit serious competence in these five crucial areas. Those that do find they can not only respond effectively to the daily demands arising from engaging in public debate, but also make a very significant impact on how large numbers of people think and act.

The best campaigns know who they need to move in order to win, the right messages to move those people and how to physically reach them. They are able to take the right decisions time after time to ensure that people actually see and hear the right messages in the media, or directly through mailings, ads or face-to-face contact. They operate as machines of influence.

Some political veterans, especially in government, are fatalistic about the outcome of elections and political debate in general. They display a *seen it all before* mentality and a cynical world-weariness about their ability to change anything. These people are not only irritating in the extreme but they are wrong. The best campaigns really can change the outcome of elections and political debates.

APPLYING CAMPAIGN SKILLS IN BUSINESS

The massive growth of opinion online demands businesses put people first. They have to forget the old ways of communicating – the focus on advertising, marketing and elite media relations – and instead turn their attention to affecting the public conversation taking place about them. That demands prioritising the mastery of this mix of skills in pure communications as well as the mechanics.

Some businesses will be sceptical about their need to focus on some of these skills, doubting their relevance to affecting public opinion or the extent to which campaigns really utilise them when they receive such scant attention in the media. Such businesses might decide to search for the magic bullet to deal with the problems they face, looking first and foremost to improve their web capabilities.

In a world where businesses are exposed to opinion that is mostly on the web, improving web capabilities is important. It will help enormously to enable staff to develop skills in Facebook page design, web video production, blogging, making the most of Twitter, and a million other skills associated with competent web use.

But, ultimately, while skills in these tactical areas are important, maximising them depends on developing expertise in people and what makes them tick. At the end of this book I give some specific recommendations for how businesses can manage their reputation online, as well as in the media and in the regular crises that firms face in this new world. The bulk of this book, though, focuses on the fundamental skills I have set out in this chapter.

Those businesses that master these skills will be in an extremely strong place to start leading the public conversation on their organisation and the issues that matter to them. The web and media skills that they have in place – and that they go on to develop or buy in – will be put to excellent use. Conversely, those businesses that focus first on technology will find the emotional and aggressive conversation taking place a difficult one to enter into, and impossible to lead.

CHAPTER THREE
TESTING AND TARGETING

THE SCIENCE OF CAMPAIGNS

IN THE LAST decade, political campaigns have taken an increasingly professional and scientific approach to public persuasion for two reasons. First, in the US particularly, the electorate has polarised and the outcomes of the biggest races are increasingly close. Campaigns realise success or failure is determined by tiny numbers of identifiable voters, incentivising the development of innovative methods to increase turnout.

Second, as a result of better web technology, campaigns can more accurately target specific groups of people on a reasonable budget. Even the smallest campaigns have access to cheap and effective online databases, social media platforms and publishing facilities. What only major investment could have secured a decade ago is now possible for a relatively small amount of money.

Campaigns have become more scientific in three primary areas: opinion research; voter targeting and mobilisation; and the development of campaign *metrics* that measure progress. Together, these allow campaigns to find out what different groups of people think, how their attitudes can be shifted and whether the campaign is successful in doing so.

Terry Nelson, who was the political director of the successful Bush-Cheney 2004 Presidential campaign and founder of one of

Washington's best communications firms, FP1 Strategies, argues these three areas are integral to the success of modern campaigns:

> "Campaigns are regularly measuring standing and the effectiveness of their messaging in the polls on a regular basis. Polling has become a very important part of any campaign, which will surprise no one. Focus groups are becoming increasingly important in any budget with a sizable campaign. Targeting has always been critical.

> "But both parties have increased the sophistication of their targeting since the 2004 presidential campaign. At that point, Republicans are regarded as having the better methods. But the Democrats have improved on the GOP effort by layering in additional online data. This has given them an advantage in targeting their messages to receptive and persuadable voters, whether on or off line."[13]

While the best businesses are highly scientific with advertising and marketing, they are strangely reluctant to be so in corporate communications and public affairs – areas that can have just as large an effect on their future. Opinion research is used sporadically by even the biggest companies and agencies. Similarly, targeting is at best an afterthought and metrics in an earned media setting are largely unheard of.

In my view this approaches malpractice by the PR industry – especially given the rapid growth in relatively cheap technology, the increased understanding of how campaigns are using this approach and the growth of opinion online. It is unforgiveable not to take a rigorous, scientific approach to PR.

In the rest of this chapter I will deal with research, targeting and metrics in turn. However, it is important to remember they are intertwined and should be considered in the round – as a general cultural shift towards a more scientific and professional approach to communications.

THE IMPORTANCE OF RESEARCH IN CAMPAIGNS

Opinion research has been an integral part of political campaigns for decades. The quality of research is a key determinant in whether a campaign wins or loses. The more research a campaign does, the better placed it is to move public opinion to win.

Research is critical because campaigns do not have another method to reliably judge what people think about developing issues or about the character of a candidate. Many in politics make it their job to stay in touch with public attitudes by talking regularly to voters and monitoring issues that come up in correspondence. However, since politics is such a niche issue in most people's lives, activists and the hyper-interested have a disproportionately loud voice and campaign staff can find themselves out of touch if they do not regularly consult research.

Anthony Wells, an associate director at British pollsters YouGov and author of the influential *UK Polling Report* blog, says:

> "Research should be a deciding factor in any campaign –
> most campaigns are ultimately about changing opinion,
> whether it is public opinion, elite opinion, or the opinion
> of policymakers. It should go almost without saying that
> it is impossible to effectively change opinion if you can't
> measure what it is to begin with, if you don't know what
> beliefs, knowledge and values drive it and underlie it and
> how effective your actions are being in changing it. It is
> possible to campaign without research but you are doing
> it blindfolded."[14]

Even a savvy politician or campaign manager will find it difficult to judge what people will think about important but complicated issues like banking reform or trade policy. Very often in politics, there is no choice but to research.

Research will become even more important to campaigns in the future. This is partly due to the polarisation of politics and the need to understand what makes voters *swing*. It is also due to wider changes taking place in society. With the mainstream media in decline and a fracturing of popular culture, the public are set to become exposed to very different commentaries on the state of the country and therefore to develop very different views on the causes of major policy challenges and their solutions.

In the past, when a large section of the public read the same national and local newspapers, watched the same nightly news bulletins, and saw the same popular TV programmes, you could assume people were hearing the same stories and cultural references. This is no longer the case and it will become even more important to work out not only what is on people's minds but also how to make them understand and care about a set of issues.

HOW CAMPAIGNS USE RESEARCH

Research is integral to every serious campaign, but each will use it in its own particular way. However, there are three main uses for research: to work out *what* should be said, *how* it should be said and *who* it should be said to.

WHAT SHOULD BE SAID

In thinking about what to say, few campaigns use research to design an entire policy agenda. Rather, they will use research to work out which parts of their policy platform should be amplified and which played down. Most candidates will, after all, have a record and cannot credibly invent new positions on every policy and a completely new approach to the world. Nor should they.

That said, if one campaign has used polling seriously to determine what they should be saying to the outside world, it is President Clinton's pre-1996 reelection campaign. With the Democrats wiped out in the 1994 mid-terms by the Republicans' simple "less government" message, Clinton's own reputation was seriously damaged and a Republican take over of the White House in 1996 looked a distinct possibility.

At this point, Clinton took on consultant Dick Morris to chart a course to rescue his Presidency and put him back on track for reelection. A monumental research operation produced a Clinton commitment to a balanced budget – in the face of opposition from left-leaning Democrats – and also the *Values Agenda*, a research-driven campaign that saw Clinton take high-profile positions on a series of moral issues facing the US and develop programmes to deal with them.

Running from the end of 1995, the campaign was extremely popular with the electorate (above all, with crucial swing voters), and put Clinton firmly on the front foot, paving the way for victory in 1996.[15]

HOW IT SHOULD BE SAID

Using research to consider how best to sell an approach to the public is much more common and is generally seen as being a much more appropriate way of using research. This is not about coming up with specific policy ideas and positioning, but working out the best way of framing an issue to the public – i.e. working out the language that should be used to describe an issue and how to present it overall. This really matters. Express a policy idea in one way and people hate it; change the language and they like it.

For example, when I worked at the No campaign against the euro – a campaign obsessed with opinion research – we knew that saying "replace the pound with the euro" was much more effective with voters than saying "join the euro". This was partly because of the emotional attachment some people had to the pound and because some thought Britain could join the euro and keep the pound at the same time.

Campaign literature therefore talked about replacing the pound and campaign spokespeople said the same. There was no difference in the meaning of the words, but the language produced different results.

In British politics, a starker example is the difference in results you get between making a positive case for public sector reform – arguing that the private sector is more efficient – and a negative case – arguing politicians cannot be trusted to run anything because they are incompetent. Again, while there is ultimately no difference in what is being proposed, calling for politicians to be stripped of power is always very popular.

WHO IT SHOULD BE SAID TO

Finally, and this is especially ingrained in US politics, campaigns use opinion research to plan their voter targeting. Typically this involves extensive research to segment audiences into different groups that receive a particular set of messages designed to appeal to them and make them more likely to turn out to vote.

Research designed to help campaigns segment the population for micro targeting is becoming more and more important and is probably the most significant innovation in the use of research over the last two decades. It not only helps campaigns move certain groups of voters but improves their efficiency too. Money is always limited in campaigns and time even more so. Campaigns must be as efficient as possible and target their messages accordingly.

Anthony Wells of YouGov argues this has become easier with the increase in online polling:

> "The gradual shift towards online research has obvious implications in terms of cost, speed and sheer volume of data that campaigners can access – it can be done much quicker and much faster – and there is the potential for access to large banks of panel data (from both pollsters and other large banks of consumer data) that can be analysed and interrogated to identify key swing groups and segments."[16]

UNDERTAKING OPINION RESEARCH

Opinion research generates two types of data about what people think: *quantitative data* (numbers) and *qualitative data* (usually words). Generally speaking, quantitative data is generated by polls, conducted through telephone interviews or online questionnaires, or a mix of the two. Qualitative data is generated by in-depth discussions with people, usually face to face in focus groups or through in-depth one-to-one interviews.

Most campaigns will generate both types of data over the course of their work. This is because quantitative data tells you *what* voters are thinking and qualitative data tells you *why*.

For example, a poll can tell you 75% of people oppose a new tax, but the explanations generated for that could only ever be as good as the options laid out by the pollster in a list. Qualitative data taken from conversations with real people might suggest the 75% figure reflected people's belief this government would spend the revenue on niche priorities – something that might never have been picked up by a poll.

Campaigns usually focus on working out what ordinary voters think – the mass of the public that take *some* interest in political issues but who do not live for politics. Campaigns find polling to be extremely useful in probing what a representative sample of the electorate think about issues familiar to them and what issues they have clear views on. The data will be reliable because people have enough sense of the issues to give meaningful answers that probably will not change with more information.

When issues are new or complex, quantitative data can be unreliable. Where the views of ordinary voters are not formed or settled, small changes to the language of a question significantly changes results in these types of polls. You could not assume you understood public opinion in such a scenario.

FOCUS GROUPS

With these concerns about quantitative data in mind, many campaigns look to generate additional explanatory, *qualitative* data, through focus groups. Some in the media are sceptical about the merits of focus groups. They argue focus groups are used merely to hear what people are saying so campaigns can parrot back the same arguments, or they are just *eight people in a room* and therefore wildly unreliable.

These concerns fundamentally misunderstand what focus groups are for. In reality, they allow campaigns to hold conversations on new and complex issues that might require explanation to bring people up to speed to form a view on an issue. This deals with the problems that arise from simply providing people with a minimal amount of information in closed questions in standard polls.

Focus groups also give campaigns an indication of what the public have seen or heard on important issues and allow them to probe their first responses. This gives a sense for which aspects of a story have been received by voters and why. This is much more difficult to do through standard polling, which requires the use of prompts to get answers.

Focus groups also give campaigns a sense for the language they should use when developing a particular policy. Someone in a focus group always describes an issue better than campaign staff, or comes up with a new argument. In almost every focus group I have watched or moderated, I invariably came out with a better way of explaining a difficult concept because someone in the group – who previously knew next to nothing about the issue – managed to sum up exactly what we had been trying to say.

Other sceptics suggest focus groups create an unnatural and unrealistic climate that makes people say things they otherwise would not. Critics argue most people would never have a 90-minute conversation about politics and never have a serious conversation about, say, government debt. Similarly, they argue the moderator may educate the group to an unrealistic extent, creating a more informed discussion than would ever exist in the real world.

These are fair comments but mainly act as warnings to ensure groups are moderated well. Any method can be ruined by incompetence. The moderator must ensure he or she does little talking and leaves people to discuss autonomously. When a certain level of education is necessary to provoke a discussion, the moderator must ensure the level of education is only the equivalent of basic media reports. And obviously the data from groups is explanatory, not scientific.

HOW TECHNOLOGY IS CHANGING RESEARCH

OPENING UP NEW METHODS

Developments in technology and science continue to change the nature of opinion research, and campaigns continue to make greater strides in understanding public opinion. Just as phone research cut costs by ending the need for large numbers of research staff in the field, online technology is cutting costs even further by removing even more people from the job of distributing polls and processing results.

This allows campaigns to do even more research and also to reach those voters who have always been more difficult to track down, namely younger voters. Online research also allows for a greater range of material to be tested, such as visual material, which is obviously unsuitable for phone polling.

Improvements in technology and changes in lifestyle will continue to revolutionise the sector. For example, for some time better-funded campaigns have been making use of dial groups, which are larger focus groups where people watch audiovisual material while turning a dial up or down to register support or opposition to visual messages. Such research is useful in probing people's responses to emotional visual messages, where people give an instinctive reaction to what they are seeing and hearing, and also their instinctive responses to the human characteristics they immediately see in candidates (their appearance, manner, voice and so on).

This is only the beginning. In the next couple of decades, campaigns will use our increased understanding of the brain to make more use of *neuromarketing*, where researchers test the responses of people's brains to written messages and audiovisual imagery. Given increased evidence from brain research that the best way of influencing people is through emotional messages delivered visually, neuromarketing will unquestionably become common in the future.

In the next chapter I will explain more about what cognitive science teaches us about the messages that affect people. For now, it is important to understand that one of the results of our increased understanding that people are moved particularly by emotional messaging is a greater focus from research firms on the importance of values and character in determining what people feel about issues. This is vital in campaigns and for businesses.

VALUES AND CHARACTER

It is still largely the case that polling data is presented to the outside world, and to most average clients, with data split by characteristics such as favoured party, age, gender, socio-economic grouping (traditionally known as social class) and region of residence.

Clearly, pollsters cannot split the results by every conceivable characteristic as the results would take up too much room. In some circumstances, though, it might make more sense to split people's views on issues by their values and character, rather than by their age and gender, for example. It certainly makes sense for campaigns to probe issues of values and character in their polling to help them design their best emotional pitch.

Bill Clinton's successful Values Agenda campaign was clearly a heavily emotional pitch – it dug deeply into the American public's values and character. In *The Power of the Vote*, Douglas Schoen, one of Clinton's polling team under Dick Morris, explains how the campaign did this: "Using a modified Myers-Briggs personality test, we sought to classify the electorate by personality traits; extroversion versus introversion, sensing versus intuition, thinking versus feeling, and judging versus perceiving."

The questions they asked included such unconventional questions as "Are you the life of the party or a wallflower?" and "Do you value common sense or a vision?"

At this point, having developed a real sense for the various personality types in the electorate, they probed lifestyle choices – everything from what TV shows people watched, to their favourite sports, to their views on others' life choices.[17]

This operation allowed the Clinton campaign to develop a phenomenal understanding of the electorate and, above all, crucial swing voters. They developed a sense for which issues they should focus on and also how they should pitch their approach to these issues. They also got a strong sense for how they should appeal emotionally to voters because they understood what was actually behind voters' views on the world.

In practical terms, too, they found out where they should place their advertising to reach the right people. Dick Morris believes that their early advertising campaign – a long way out from the November 1996 election – was a determining factor in Clinton's eventual success.[18]

HOW BUSINESSES CAN USE RESEARCH

GREATER USE OF ISSUES-BASED RESEARCH IS NEEDED

There are too many businesses who pour money into consumer research but who remain reluctant to extend research budgets to their corporate communications and public affairs teams. Many businesses are therefore signing off very large communications campaigns – with very large budgets – with no real sense for how they will play out.

Andrew Hawkins, the chairman of the increasingly powerful ComRes research agency in London, which has conducted research for some of the world's biggest firms, provides an explanation:

> "Many more businesses today than ever before use research to help steer their public position on issues, but it is still a minority activity. I believe there are three principal reasons for this. First, this type of research is relatively novel; I recall managing the first-ever panel of MPs for a lobbying company back in the early 1990s, and subsequently setting up the second one, but this type of research was very much in its infancy back then.
>
> "Second, those few corporate communications [teams] which actually have research budgets nevertheless do not have the purchasing power of their marketing or advertising colleagues. This is slowly changing, although regulatory change can have just as much impact on a company's performance as poor marketing. And senior managers, those setting budgets, also need to be persuaded of the value of research to support external communications.
>
> "Third, purchasing or advising on the purchase of research is very often the domain of in-house market research professionals, but they can often have little awareness of how research of this type would help support a company's involvement in public debate. Again this is changing – as quickly as we can push it – but it requires time."[19]

The change in corporate attitudes towards issues-based research must accelerate. The explosion of opinion demands all major businesses become experts in public opinion. Businesses need a deep understanding of what people think about them and their key issues if they are going to influence these people and exploit the opportunities that exist.

While many businesses have an instinctive grasp of what the public thinks about the sorts of goods and services they sell – after all, they will have access to detailed sales figures – fewer firms will have a proper sense for what the public thinks about them as an organisation. Fewer still will have a sense for what the public thinks about those issues that affect their business, such as the approach of politicians to regulating their sector. As a rule, the more research a business conducts, the better it will be able to move opinion.

As a bare minimum, businesses need to conduct landscape research projects once a year to work out what the public thinks about their sector and possible changes within it. This will give their communications teams the confidence to know their public communications are hitting home. Ideally, businesses should conduct extensive tracking polls on how attitudes are changing towards the sector and on key issues that affect them, supplemented by regular focus groups that explain why the public are thinking what they are.

Businesses feeling the effects of the developing public conversation about them can use research like campaigns to work out:

1. what people think about them and their key issues;

2. how best to position themselves in their market and how to approach key issues; and

3. how best to segment their audiences in order to target their messages better.

A FAST FOOD CHAIN UNDER FIRE

Let us consider a couple of hypothetical scenarios. Firstly, a fast food chain has come in for public criticism from a high-profile politician for supposedly deliberately targeting children with its advertising. Online media outlets and NGOs in the food sector are stirring up a major debate on social media platforms. The business knows its reputation is vulnerable and there is a threat of further regulation. What should their response be?

First, the restaurant chain should produce an opinion poll on the evening of the politician's speech. Polling firms can sometimes get the results from their polls back within a day, particularly if the sample size is small. The poll should probe the extent to which the public agreed with the politician fundamentally, or thought the speech was overblown.

This would be done with a few open questions on the big themes the politician laid out – such as whether the government had any role intervening on public health issues and whether the government should stay out of people's lives – before asking for responses to a set of arguments for and against what the politician was saying. Finally, the poll would set out a series of remedies the restaurant chain could take in response. This might include pulling all even remotely controversial ads, or setting out ways to heighten the powers of an independent regulator.

Such a poll would give the restaurant chain the following: a sense for whether the public backed the politician on points of key principle, such as whether it was accurate that the chain actually *was* marketing to kids; how much they cared; and whether they believed it was right for politicians to intervene. It would give a sense for whether the chain should pull the ads and others like it and also guide the chain's policy response moving forward. It would help to guide the business' public comment and its corresponding action.

From my own experience, the British public are interventionist when it comes to government regulation, particularly where it regards children. Almost certainly, whatever the merits of the specific points made by the politician, the public would line up against the restaurant. The public is generally hostile to all advertising where children are concerned. The chain might therefore find itself using the poll to phrase its near-apology and to come up with a set of policy responses that would move it back towards popular opinion.

Too many businesses mess up this response because they do not test it first, and because what they say is unclear. Many firms are prone to hedging or giving robust responses they then alter, which only adds fuel to the fire in the media and online. The business should be looking to develop a clear line that it does not move from. Research tells you what that clear line should be.

A BANK IN THE WAKE OF THE FINANCIAL CRISIS

Let us imagine a second scenario. A high street bank wants to improve its public reputation in the aftermath of the financial crisis. The bank traditionally had a perfectly reasonable reputation but was dragged down by the crisis, even though it did not have a significant investment banking arm. It was not one of the poster boys of the crisis but its senior executives came in for occasional criticism for their salaries. Furthermore, the bank was mentioned in parliament for not doing enough to help small businesses.

Initially, the bank should conduct a detailed landscape poll and set of focus groups to work out what the public thinks in detail about the financial sector in general, the bank specifically and the key issues that affect both. This might include research into whether people blame banks rather than politicians for the financial crisis, the extent high street banks are put in the same bracket as investment banks, how much the public really know and care about the high salaries of senior executives in the banking sector, and what people think the main jobs of the banks are and how well they are doing these jobs.

They would then run a separate research programme to test the overall approach and specific messages that would persuade people to be more sympathetic. This could build on the findings of the preliminary research. They would offer a series of pro-bank messages likely to appeal to people, run using *split samples* (i.e. different sets) of people against a single anti-bank *control* message. This would allow the bank to work out which of the messages played out best against a generic hostile message. The bank could then probe the meaning behind these messages in a few more focus groups.

The research would ensure that there were significant numbers of additional useful questions to probe issues like people's lifestyle, values and media habits so that the bank could build up an accurate picture of the types of people who hold different views.

This would allow the bank to segment its audience to target its communications campaign. For example, the bank might find it had a particular problem with middle-class, free-market-sceptic women and might conclude the answer was an earned media campaign in the quality press designed to amplify their CSR (corporate social responsibility) programme. This may well be what these particular women care most about.

Let us assume the research showed anger directed towards banks was general rather than specific and the public did not understand the causes of the financial crisis or where blame lay. It revealed general anger towards the very high salaries of senior executives. It would probably also show that, overwhelmingly, the public thought the job of banks was to provide a service to members of the public and small businesses to help them go about their lives – and that banks should focus their policy and communications efforts here. This is a plausible scenario from the dozens of polls on the subject I have read.

The bank would then conclude there was little merit in trying to address public anger over the financial crisis and high salaries and bonuses. Rather, they should focus on starting a new public conversation on their improved customer service and policies on public and small business lending. They would also realise certain types of people would never listen to them and they should focus most on trying to communicate with their customer base and interested members of the public that were politically unaligned and willing to listen.

This bank would be in an infinitely stronger position to construct a campaign to improve its public reputation. This bank would know what people thought about it and why. It would know which messages moved specific groups of people and how best to reach them.

Tied together with additional desk research on what people were saying on the web and social media platforms, this would completely transform the bank's ability to affect its own reputation. Such projects are not cheap but, costing in the very low tens of thousands of pounds, they are chicken feed for a multinational bank with a serious PR problem.

TARGETING MESSAGES

HOW TARGETING IS USED

In the 1980s and 1990s, political campaigns worried overwhelmingly about the creation of two or three key messages to appeal to the bulk of the population. Direct mail and direct voter contact played a role in appealing to voters with particular concerns, but these operations were relatively expensive and logistically difficult. The development of the web and online databases and the massive increase in available data has transformed the ability of campaigns to target specific groups cheaply and effectively.

Targeting is used in two main ways. Firstly, to create sets of different messages. Campaigns use research, grassroots intelligence and data like voters' consumer habits, or voting record, to segment the public into specific target audiences. They then create campaign themes and messages designed to appeal to as many of these groups as realistically possible, but without losing clarity or distinctiveness. Campaigns know they cannot appeal to everyone, so they develop themes that hit the most likely to move.

The second use is to get the right people to vote – either to vote in principle, or for a particular candidate. These campaigns are often done quietly in the form of direct mail, email and very targeted advertising on social media platforms, niche TV channels, or niche publications. They are designed with small numbers of people in mind and usually focus on a very specific message designed to reflect a group's known values or interests. This approach is known as *micro targeting*.

This might seem like a distinction without a difference but one is about creating public messages designed to appeal to significant sections of the population, while the other is about the creation of messages designed to be heard *only* by a small group of people. Both, however, are about moving known groups and are about increasing the impact and efficiency of the campaign.

George Bush's 2004 presidential campaign team were the real pioneers of this approach – this campaign deserves particular attention from those seeking to learn lessons from the campaign world. They accumulated so much data on the electorate and target groups that they were able to develop an extremely sophisticated understanding of the lifestyle and consumer choices of likely voters. For example, they knew that Republicans were more likely to drink certain drinks, watch certain sports and so on. Micro targeted ad campaigns were developed to speak to exactly the right people.

As political director, Terry Nelson was responsible for the Bush campaign's grassroots operation. He explained to me the importance of targeting to the success of their operation:

> "In 2004, we used micro targeting in every targeted state. This process had been tested in a few smaller campaigns in 2002 and by the RNC [Republican National Committee] in 2003.
>
> "Micro targeting combined two databases. The first was the RNC voter database, which contained basic information about each voter, as well as any information that we had learned about that voter through standard canvassing techniques. The second database used was a consumer database, which tracked stated consumer preferences as well as information that can be publicly tracked – like whether the consumer is a home owner. With the combined databases, a large sample survey is conducted in each state. From that, the research team would determine the important factors that might dictate

a political opinion or belief, and then how to segment the file beyond those who had been survey respondents.

"We found this technique to be extraordinarily valuable in targeting voters who, in the past, may not have been selected in our standard targeting efforts. This was especially true in states without voter registration, like Ohio, or with voters who were not registered by party. It also allowed us to target voters generally with the issues in which they were most interested. Thus, with our base voters, we could target social or economic conservatives appropriately and with persuadable voters we could deliver a message in which we were highly confident."[20]

Sasha Issenberg, author of *The Victory Lab*, a superb book on the science behind modern campaigns, has written extensively about the Obama campaign's efforts to build on the work of the Bush campaign. There seems no doubt that – under the Obama campaign's leadership – the Democrats have now overtaken the Republicans in the sophistication of their targeting operation.

Issenberg points out that the Obama campaigns made huge use of direct contact with the American public, asking people how they would vote and the likelihood of them voting in the first place. They found that these simple, even obvious, pieces of information were extremely useful in helping to target campaign resources. In other words, Obama's team was using old-fashioned, voter-contact methods to supplement the existing information they had on voters. This allowed them to improve their Get Out The Vote operation.[21]

Campaigns therefore create an approach that accurately segments the electorate into specific groups, and then develops messages designed to influence and mobilise those voters. As our understanding of the human brain increases, along with better and cheaper technology, it is possible to imagine extremely personal and persuasive messages pushed out to very small groups of people. While campaigns may not be able to target *individuals* on a massive scale any time soon, it cannot be that far away.

HOW BUSINESSES SHOULD CONSIDER THEIR OWN TARGETING

MICRO TARGETING OF CONSUMERS

Campaigns cannot claim to have pioneered the approach to targeting. Without doubt, firms in the commercial world were the real pioneers of micro targeting from a sales perspective. The direct marketing guru Lester Wunderman covers this approach in his book *Being Direct*.[22] Businesses have long been using their vast consumer databanks to develop marketing campaigns. Think about the sophistication of the marketing operations of modern British supermarkets and you see this approach in action.

While businesses have used this targeted approach in marketing and advertising, only a minority have transferred this into general corporate communications and public affairs operations. I have worked with some businesses that have produced audience segmentation of a sophistication that could stand comparison with the most competent campaigns, but most are a long way off.

The nature of the public debate means most people engaged in it will be completely different to those people businesses normally deal with. For example, many of those actively engaged in debate on banking regulation – people who in part shape the reputation of banks – are motivated by politics and ethics rather than worries about the safety of their savings.

Businesses have to think about research in a different way to deal with this, expanding their intelligence to include a broader set of people. In doing so, like campaigns, they must develop a sense for the public as a whole before narrowing in on those most important to the debate about their operations. This research must be matched with their own desk research – and their own general experience – of the sort of people that seem most active in discussing them on the web.

Terry Nelson believes others can learn lessons from the approach taken by campaigns:

"In our case, we had underserved voters – voters who should be voting for us, but who were not properly motivated – and persuadable voters, who needed to hear the right message from us to vote our way. Finding these voters was a significant factor in our 2004 victory.

"But these kinds of people exist everywhere, not just in political campaigns. The key to a successful public affairs campaign is finding the right message to persuade people to take some action. But I also think that the micro targeting project was a paradigm shift in politics. It exposed a whole group of voters who could be turned out, who had not been actively targeted in the past. Of course, this kind of change in approach can be very consequential in any campaign, if you are open to it."[23]

Andrew Hawkins of ComRes also argues corporate targeting is possible and vital:

"Message targeting is a vital extension of a company's marketing, even if the audiences are vastly different (which is seldom the case in any event – politicians are consumers too). It is increasingly apparent that there is a seamless continuum between different interest groups, such as consumers, investors, regulators, and employees. Even those who are not consumers are influencers."[24]

What does this mean in practice? Hawkins provides an example:

"Take food safety – mums, and especially affluent ones, are of disproportionate importance as consumers but also as news narrowcasters at the school gate or on sites like Mumsnet. Moreover, their influence in many markets is exacerbated by their political importance (ironically of course the opposite used to be the case). Yet without knowing how political messages play out with this audience, a company risks missing out on or even alienating a vital lever in wider public policy debates. The corporate landscape is littered with examples, such as the large proportion of consumers who try to boycott brands associated with tax avoidance. The political is the commercial – it is as simple and direct a relationship as that."[25]

More thoughtful and efficient targeting has been a viable option for campaigns and businesses for some time, particularly with the proliferation of polling. However, the development of social media over the last five years opens up massive new possibilities.

UTILISING SOCIAL MEDIA

The biggest companies can use extensive polling operations and their vast banks of consumer data to run huge operations that appeal to large numbers of people across social media platforms. But the relative ease of targeting on social media, and the relatively low cost, means even very small organisations can create very targeted campaigns. By thinking hard about the type of people they have traditionally appealed to, and those they would like to appeal to in the future, virtually any organisation has the ability to significantly improve its efficiency.

In *Likeable Social Media*, Dave Kerpen explains what this means for businesses:

"On Facebook alone, you could target people based on their age, gender, education, marital status, interests, job title, and employer. For example, instead of a beer company searching for men aged 21 to 34, the company could easily find those 21- to 23-year-old males in key geographic markets who list 'drinking', 'partying', or 'bars' as interests on their profiles."[26]

He adds:

"In the past, newspapers, magazines, television, and radio allowed marketers to tap into wide audiences of people, based around broad demographic criteria: 18- to 34-year-olds, 25- to 54-year-old females, or males 55 and older in New York, for example. But in hindsight, in almost every case, these categories were too sweeping. Specifics will help you hone in on your target audience, connecting you directly with the consumer. For instance, are you targeting parents or singles? Sports fans? Hockey fans only? Are you in every major market or only certain markets?"[27]

A high street fashion chain's sourcing is questioned

Let us take a hypothetical scenario. Imagine a major high street fashion chain worries about criticism it takes regarding the sourcing of its clothes. The firm has been criticised for using cheap labour in the Far East and the occasional stories that have appeared in the left-leaning media recently have started to fuel criticism online. A Facebook page calling for a boycott has been around for some time and there are regular bursts of activity on Twitter backing a boycott.

The business knows its customers are primarily women in their late teens to early thirties and are mostly lower middle class / upper working class. They know most coverage in the media comes and goes with little impact on sales because most of their customers do not read the newspapers or watch the main bulletins. However, they know that criticism in consumer magazines affects sales somewhat, as do social media campaigns, particularly when they are backed by relatively well-known and respected people – celebrities and better-known commentators.

The business concludes there is no point trying to defend their working practices directly to their customers. They might decide that while customers take an interest in what well-known people are saying, these customers actually have little interest in the facts. The business might therefore try to target the ultimate sources of the negative stories in consumer magazines and online.

Here the business might conclude that the ultimate source of these stories were well-educated, left-leaning, younger women, whose comments on social media were being picked up by other influential young people in the media, politics and in the NGO world. These younger women are therefore the primary target for the business to explain why things were not quite as they seemed and that their record was positive.

The business might therefore decide to run a major social media campaign, targeting advertising on these younger women to set the record straight. They might produce a simple Facebook ad called 'Our Record With Suppliers', which would be visible to those women that checked the relevant boxes on Facebook highlighting their political leanings, their age and so on.

This ad might take them through to a dedicated page on their own site, that might in turn include a link back to their website which showed a short film on their labour practices. There might also be a short and simple rebuttal document or links to endorsements from people these young women might trust. In addition, the business might seek to generate coverage on websites known to be popular with their target audience.

Whatever was decided upon, this targeted approach would be much more likely to see them affect their overall coverage than if they had just tried to push back across the board using ads in magazines, and generating stories and features in the mainstream media. It would also be much, much cheaper than taking this more traditional approach.

MEASURING PROGRESS THROUGH METRICS

METRICS ENTER THE MAINSTREAM

The best book on the use of metrics in the corporate sphere is Michael Lewis' *Moneyball*,[28] which looks at the Oakland Athletics baseball team's use of statistics and metrics to choose their new players and to measure progress.

As Lewis shows, Athletics coach Billy Beane assembled a brilliant and cheap baseball team made up of players with excellent statistics, but whose style saw them under-appreciated by the rest of baseball. The Athletics' approach was simple – if metrics showed the guy could play, he *could* play and was bought.

It did not take long for political campaigns to catch on to the power of metrics. According to veteran Republican consultant Karl Rove, the Bush 2004 campaign were inspired by *Moneyball* to develop their own crucial data points.[29] Under Campaign Manager Ken Mehlman's influence, the campaign developed metrics in all the main constituent parts of the operation. This included more obvious places like fundraising, voter contact and voter registration, but it also included developing metrics in those areas seen as being harder to measure – namely, media coverage.

According to political journalists Mark Halperin and John Harris, these press metrics were taken seriously by the campaign:

> "Another area in which the campaign demanded not just measured results but the *right* measured results was press coverage. Mehlman did not care how many press releases were sent out; he wanted to see metrics that showed how much actual news coverage – the outputs that mattered – was garnered by those press releases. How many minutes of the local and national news were allotted to their candidate's ideas? How many headlines focused on the Republicans' message of the previous day? How many inches of text were printed in the newspapers?"[30]

As the Bush campaign showed, there are two main benefits of focusing on metrics. Firstly, they help campaigns measure and understand progress. Amid the general chaos of a political campaign, when you have both internal and external voices telling you all the time how things are going, it is critical campaigns have a set of objective measures that *prove* levels of progress one way or another.

Secondly, metrics help hold senior campaign staff to account – senior staff can see what works but also *who* works. It is important to distinguish between those that are quietly effective and those that do little but with great style.

Barack Obama's 2008 and 2012 campaigns took this obsession with data further. Sasha Issenberg explains in *The Victory Lab* that the Obama 2008 campaign generated so much data that they had to take on additional staff to come in and run special projects to get the most out of it:

> "[Obama staffer Michael] Simon introduced the kitchen cabinet [of new staff] to a largely secret stockpile of data known within the Obama campaign as the Matrix. It was a centralized repository that would gather every instance of the campaign 'touching' a voter, as field operatives like to put it, including each piece of mail, doorstep visit, and phone call, whether from a volunteer or a paid phone bank... For the general election, the Matrix was expanded to include non-targeted communication to which an individual was exposed, including broadcast and cable ads and candidate visits to their media market."[31]

The tightness of US presidential politics means the focus on ever-more sophisticated metrics will continue to grow. Campaigns know the importance of objective measurements and they have been proved useful. The use of metrics has entered the DNA of modern campaigns now, meaning that there is a *culture* of measurement, just as there is a culture of testing. That means there is no barrier standing in the way of those that want to take the use of metrics to the next level.

There is an important caveat to all this. Metrics are designed to help organisations run effective campaigns and are not ends in themselves. The creation and monitoring of key metrics must not become a standalone industry that ends up adding vast layers of bureaucracy. For some organisations, reluctant as I am to admit this, there may come a time when they have too much information.

Organisations must ensure that they are measuring what is really important – and they should only extend their system of metrics as far as they can without adversely affecting their view of the world and their decision-taking capability.

Similarly, organisations must also ensure metrics do not end up creating perverse incentives, for example where staff end up working to create endless *hits* in the media, but which are objectively not of high value. Thinking hard in advance about the type of metrics is important, but it is also important that organisations have a regular reality check to ask whether or not metrics are really helping.

BUSINESS' USE OF METRICS

As technology improves and becomes cheaper, and as campaigns become more experienced, the use and understanding of metrics will grow. Presidential campaigns and some of the more sophisticated Senate campaigns in the US will lead the way, having the money to invest and desire created by the need to win. Other campaigns will reap some of the benefits of this developing approach.

Most businesses engaged in public debate will not need a system of metrics even remotely along the lines of the presidential campaigns. Businesses are not trying to win votes, but simply affect opinion. However, corporate communications teams should still accept the fundamental lessons of campaign metrics and apply them. As set out above, the widespread use of metrics enables an organisation to measure progress, to hold staff to account and ultimately to set targets for people to meet. Metrics are an essential management tool.

What data should businesses seek to generate and what should they try to measure? The frustrating answer to both of these questions is that it depends on what the firm is trying to achieve and what its strategy is for achieving its objectives. There is no off-the-shelf system for generating and analysing data. Businesses, like campaigns, have to generate their own systems.

Some of this will come easily. Online campaigns can be measured simply using tools the business will already have access to. For example, businesses will be able to measure Facebook likes, Twitter followers, website visits, and so on, at virtually no cost and very quickly. Other tools allow businesses to measure the number of times emails have been opened, or the number of times links embedded in the emails have been clicked on.

When obvious metrics have been set, it is down to businesses to create their own. Some businesses might measure simple things like the number of stories the communications team generates from scratch, or the number of quotes that push a particular message, or the number of broadcast interviews the chief executive does in a given period. Useful metrics might also include the number of people who join the business' online campaign to pressure the government to cut taxes, or the number of emails sent to politicians, or the number of tear-off forms sent back to the business pledging support on a particular issue.

It would not be right to imply it does not matter what metrics a business generates – some will be more useful than others. Yet it is true there is no set of guidelines to help businesses in this process. The most important thing is asking fundamental questions of what would genuinely measure progress. It is obviously also crucial the business then *acts* upon the data generated – that metrics become a key part of the culture of the operation.

THE BENEFITS OF THE SCIENTIFIC APPROACH

The exposure of so many businesses to the public has injected real uncertainty into the corporate communications world. More scrutiny, more emotional commentary from the public and a faster pace all make life difficult and more like campaigns.

This near chaos demands firms try to bring about a degree of order. Some might say this is wishful thinking and the nature of the explosion of opinion is that it will always be uncertain and chaotic. There is some truth to this. There is a limit to how much businesses will ever be able to control the debate on their organisation and issues.

That said, the effects for businesses will be worse if they do not at least *try* to bring some order to the debate surrounding them. They need to study political campaigns and take this more scientific approach. Such an approach will make them more effective at working out what they should be saying publicly and who to. It will also allow them to work out the effects they are having as they go about navigating public debate.

The best businesses – and therefore the best communications agencies – will go one further and demand everything is seriously tested, that all communications are clearly targeted at key audiences and that metrics are used to measure progress. Businesses that do not adopt this approach will underperform and agencies that do not adopt this approach will rightly lose market share.

CHAPTER FOUR
MESSAGES THAT MOVE PEOPLE

WINNING HEARTS AND MINDS

MUNZENBERG AND THE BOLSHEVIKS

WILLI MUNZENBERG WAS arguably the greatest propagandist of the twentieth century. Having been a close friend of Lenin's during his pre-1917 exile, Munzenberg became one of the Bolsheviks' greatest assets in Europe in the 1920s and 1930s. Working from his native Berlin, Munzenberg coordinated a massive communications operation across Europe designed to promote the Soviet cause.

While Munzenberg's interests were vast – running charities, book clubs, film studios (where he helped make Sergei Eisenstein's *Battleship Potemkin* such a success), newspapers and publishing houses – he specialised in one thing above all: promoting the moral superiority of the Soviet Union by deploying respected, independent voices to make this case publicly.

Stephen Koch, who wrote about Munzenberg's work in his classic *Double Lives*, said this about him:

> "His goal was to create for the right-thinking non-communist West the dominating political prejudice of the era: the belief that any opinion that happened to serve the foreign policy of the Soviet Union was derived from the most essential elements of human decency. He wanted to instil the feeling, like a truth of nature, that seriously to

criticize or challenge Soviet policy was the unfailing mark of a bad, bigoted, and probably stupid person, while support was equally infallible proof of a forward-looking mind committed to all that was best for humanity and marked by an uplifting refinement of sensibility."[32]

Munzenberg encouraged his network of agents to recruit as many as possible to say things that boosted Soviet moral authority and undermined the moral authority of the West. Some of these people came willingly and knowingly, while others, dismissively referred to as *innocents* by Munzenberg, were recruited without knowing they had been. To Munzenberg, all that mattered was the words that came out of their mouths in public; the rest was irrelevant.

It was a simple strategy, if not an easy one to execute. But Munzenberg executed it consistently and brilliantly for nearly two decades. He not only understood the power of moral arguments in themselves, focusing particularly on the West's patchy and deteriorating record on the protection of minorities, but he understood the moral power of intellectuals and cultural icons in delivering these arguments to Western audiences.

One of Munzenberg's first operations under the Bolsheviks' developing government after the October revolution was to ensure that the American-organised famine relief effort to help Russian peasants in the early 1920s did not give the Americans too much credit. Worried about American capitalists being seen to rescue incompetent Russian communists, Lenin asked Munzenberg to develop a disaster-relief effort that was to be seen as a real workers' effort – an authentically communist response to this disaster.[33]

The Bolsheviks were keen to take American money given the dire nature of the famine, but they ensured that the masses saw the relief effort as an ideologically acceptable, communist-led one. According to Koch, who interviewed Munzenberg's former lover Babette Gross, when he asked her at what point the Soviet relief effort became primarily interested in propaganda, she answered, "At the first moment."[34]

THE POWER OF EMOTION IN POLITICS

How could Munzenberg have been so successful? After all, while Western Europe and the United States had their problems, the Soviet Union in the early 1920s was an economic mess. While its performance improved into the 1930s – certainly in relative terms as the West suffered depression – it was still a much poorer society.

What Munzenberg understood was the extreme power of *emotional* arguments in appealing to the public. Munzenberg knew that objective *facts* were less important in shaping public opinion than what people could be made to *feel* about the relative moral positions of the Soviet Union and the Western powers. In attracting significant Western support for the Soviet cause, and helping to grow the Communist Party in Germany and elsewhere, Munzenberg's operation was a case study in how emotion can trump reason in political debate.

Then, as now, most people want to feel they are morally good. It is important they feel this themselves but it is important to them that others see them as good too. This is not to suggest that people are cynical – most people *are* generally good and try to behave in the right way for the right reasons – it is just that they wish to see this in themselves and have others see it in them too.

Writing as Munzenberg was having such success – in his 1921 book *Public Opinion* – American political commentator Walter Lippmann noted the emotional power of moral behaviour. He wrote:

> "There are people who are insensitive to facts, and aroused only by ideas. But though the emotion is aroused by the idea, we are unable to satisfy the emotion by acting ourselves upon the scene itself. The idea of the starving Russian child evokes a desire to feed the child. But the person so aroused cannot feed it. He can only give money to an impersonal organization, or to a personification which he calls Mr Hoover.

"His money does not reach that child. It goes to a general pool from which a mass of children are fed. And so just as the idea is second hand, so are the effects of the action second hand. The cognition is indirect, the conation is indirect, only the effect is immediate. Of the three parts of the process, the stimulus comes from somewhere out of sight, only the emotion exists entirely within the person. Of the child's hunger he has only an idea, of the child's relief he has only an idea, but of his own idea to help he has a real experience. It is the central fact of the business, the emotion within himself, which is first hand."[35]

For Lippmann, the act of giving was about fulfilling an emotional desire to do good. As he points out, people could not see the effects on the Russian child, and could not have any sense of how the money was spent. The only concrete effect of the act was to feel good. Again, this is not to denigrate the act at all, in fact the opposite. It shows that most people want to behave in the right way and, to use a weak phrase, be *nice*.

In a similar way, people want to believe their voting and general political choices are motivated by morality. Of course, that has its limits – at some point, for example, the trade-off between what is good for an individual and their family overtakes concerns about what is good for society as a whole.

Most people try to avoid that trade-off intellectually, preferring to vote and hold views on issues where their personal interests align with their perceptions for what is good for everyone else. Usually, what is good for individual families *will* be good for society as a whole, but sometimes people go through emotional and intellectual gymnastics to justify their views.

THE DEVELOPING USE OF EMOTIONAL ARGUMENTS

This use of emotional arguments in politics continued in the decades following Munzenberg's brilliant improvisation. With the proliferation of TV in the post-war period, and the ability of campaigns to reach people through visual means, the use of very emotional appeals really took off.

One of the greatest political ads ever made was the famous 'Daisy Ad', produced by legendary consultant Tony Schwartz for Lyndon Johnson's presidential campaigns in 1964.[36] Johnson's opponent – Barry Goldwater – was a very conservative candidate and many voters worried his aggressive approach to foreign and security policy would embroil the US in more conflicts abroad. Many thought Goldwater was extreme. Schwartz's ad tapped into these fears by powerfully but implicitly linking a Goldwater presidency with the prospect of nuclear war.

The ad began with a young child picking petals off a flower, counting upwards as she pulled each petal off. As she gets to ten, the voice of someone counting down to a missile launch kicks in and counts back down. A mushroom cloud appears amid an explosion. Lyndon Johnson then says: "These are the stakes: to make a world in which all of God's children can live, or to go into the dark. We must either love each other, or we must die." A narrator ends the ad with: "Vote for President Johnson on November 3. The stakes are too high for you to stay home."

As many people have pointed out, the ad never mentioned Barry Goldwater at all, and did not say anything explicit about foreign and security policy. But the ad was so powerful because it spoke to the audience *emotionally* – it made them *feel* something. In this instance it made them fear the prospect of nuclear war – or something awful – if they voted for Goldwater. The ad ran just once on TV but the controversy provoked was such that huge numbers of people heard about it and discussed the issues it raised.

Other famous ads have used similar techniques. In 1984, Ronald Reagan's reelection campaign produced the 'Bear Ad'.[37] This showed a bear moving around slowly in a forest, while a narrator said:

> "There is a bear in the woods. For some people, the bear
> is easy to see. Others don't see it at all. Some people say
> the bear is tame. Others say it's vicious and dangerous.

Since no one can really be sure who's right, isn't it smart
to be as strong as the bear? If there is a bear."

Again, the ad did not mention President Reagan or his opponent
Walter Mondale. It did not even mention anything specific about
defence. But the emotional message was unmistakable – Ronald
Reagan favoured a strong defence policy and by implication Walter
Mondale and the Democrats did not.

These sorts of emotional appeals are now completely integral to
modern politics. Even on issues that naturally lend themselves to a
more rational, analytical approach, campaigns still seek to move
people through emotional appeals.

For example, looking at the most recent US presidential election in
2012, where the issue of the economy was central to political debate,
President Obama's campaign focused not on concrete facts like the
relative economic performance of the US in the downturn, but on the
unfairness of Governor Mitt Romney's tax plans and how out of touch
and uncaring he was *as a person.*

One of the most effective ads President Obama's campaign ran was a
recording of Governor Romney talking about how 47% of the
electorate would never vote for him because they were dependent on
the state, laid on top of pictures of ordinary people who worked hard
but still received financial support from the government. All of this
was crucial in undermining the Romney campaign's hope that their
economic message would help carry them to victory.

Political campaigns know that their governing record or their specific
policy plans really matter in determining how people vote. A party
that presides over a major economic downturn, or a massive growth
in the crime rate, or a deterioration in healthcare, is always going to
be vulnerable. The facts matter. But it is nonetheless undeniably true
that in making their case to the electorate, campaigns know they are
better off appealing primarily to people's emotions. That does not
preclude the use of facts, but these facts need to be marshalled in such
a way as to move people.

WHY EMOTIONAL APPEALS WORK

That human beings make decisions in an emotional and irrational way is not a new discovery. Written in the middle of the nineteenth century, French social scientist Gustave Le Bon's infamous *The Crowd* was essentially a handbook for the emotional manipulation of the masses.[38] Robert Cialdini's *Influence* also provides case studies from social scientists in the middle of the twentieth century where they had managed to affect people's behaviour through, for example, types of social pressure.[39] And in his influential 1973 book, *The Responsive Chord*, Daisy Ad producer Tony Schwartz argued the big question for someone watching a politician on TV is this: "How do I feel about him?"[40]

However, two developments have occurred in recent times that give political campaigns and interested businesses greater insight into the power of emotion in shaping opinion. The first is the increased understanding we now have of how the brain works, which is slowly spreading into public consciousness (look at the popularity of Steven Pinker's recent book, *How the Mind Works*).[41] The second is the growth in academic research into how to use emotional messaging and social pressure in a political setting. These are significantly changing the way campaign consultants think about communication.

Research into the power of emotion in political messaging – and evidence of how it actually affects the brain – has really taken off in the last decade. A number of academic books have been published on this area.

The subject of emotional appeals in politics was first brought to a mainstream audience by Drew Westen, a professor of psychology at Emory University in Atlanta, Georgia. His book *The Political Brain* showed purely rational appeals in politics do not carry the same weight as emotional appeals. According to Westen:

> "We do not pay attention to arguments unless they engender our interest, enthusiasm, fear, anger, or contempt. We are not *moved* by leaders with whom we

do not feel an emotional resonance. We do not find policies worth debating if they don't touch on the emotional implications for ourselves, our families, or things we hold dear. From the standpoint of research in neuroscience, the more purely 'rational' an appeal, the less it is likely to activate the emotion circuits that regulate voting behavior."[42]

But *why* do such emotional appeals work?

THE DISPOSITIONAL SYSTEM AND THE SURVEILLANCE SYSTEM

Scientists believe the brain has two systems to help us deal with information we encounter in life. The first – the dispositional system – effectively allows us to cope with simple, non-challenging information we encounter – the things we barely register.

The second system – the surveillance system – kicks in when we come across new and unexpected information – information that generates core emotions like anxiety, fear or elation. The surveillance system makes us pay attention to something and enables us to learn and remember.[43] (These are similar to Daniel Kahneman's *System 1* – our auto-pilot approach to dealing with simple problems – and *System 2* – our approach for dealing with more complex problems that require conscious thought.[44])

In political terms, we should think about the dispositional system being triggered by political parties that speak to their voters on issues they agree with. A right-leaning party will be doing this when they run campaigns reminding voters of their new policy to extend prison sentences or to restrict immigration. A left-leaning party will be doing this when they call for higher taxes on the wealthiest to pay for better healthcare or raising of the minimum wage.

In both of these cases, the parties will likely not be extending the pool of voters who are attracted to them. Their partisan appeals will be unlikely to create swing voters. However, in triggering voters' dispositional system – their autopilot system – they will effectively be reminding their voters why they like their chosen party in the first place, and reminding them they need to turn out and vote on election day.

On the other hand, the surveillance system is triggered when voters receive new information that makes them question their existing worldview and their overall system for evaluating issues. Such appeals might be designed to make voters feel joyful, although in politics it is much more likely they will be designed to make them feel worried, nervous and anxious. Either way, these appeals are designed to make people stop and think and to seek out additional information.

In being designed to overcome existing beliefs and consider new information, these appeals help to create swing voters.[45] An example might be a Labour politician giving a speech warning that a British Conservative victory would ruin the National Health Service, and make it more likely people will get charged more for treatment. This message would appeal strongly to Labour partisans but also, for example, to older Conservative-leaning voters who rely on the NHS in their retirement. This message would turn these Conservative-leaning voters into real swing voters and make them at least consider the Labour alternative.

By making people actually *feel* something, campaigns that use emotion effectively are doing far more than just evoking a passing sensation. Rather, they are creating an actual physiological reaction that helps commit messages to long-term memory, changing the way that people receive information in the future.

Professor Doris Graber has been writing about how the brain deals with complex political messaging for some time. In *Processing Politics* she argues:

> "Visuals excel in emotion arousal compared to most nonvisual stimuli. Audiovisual stories that generate strong emotions, such as vistas of starving children or wartime destruction or reunions of long-separated relatives, are

more likely to be embedded in long-term memory and to be retained even when they are infrequently rehearsed. The reasons are largely physiological. Emotional arousal induces human bodies to release stimulants into the bloodstream that sensitize perceptions and speed reactions."[46]

In other words, campaigns that move people on particular issues, especially through visuals, will not only create an instant beneficial reaction, but a reaction so strong that they can get voters to recall similar feelings throughout a campaign.

INTENSIFYING EMOTIONAL APPEALS THROUGH VISUALS

As Professor Graber indicates, the best way to make emotional messages work is through the use of visual imagery with appropriate sound – effective audiovisuals, essentially. There are two obvious reasons why visuals are so important.

Firstly, as we have seen, people are moved emotionally by visuals and are better at *remembering* that emotion. On campaign ads, voiceovers and background music that run alongside the visuals can further heighten the power of the emotional appeal.[47] Secondly, from a purely practical perspective, the really high-traffic mainstream media news programmes are on TV. Some newspapers and news websites have big audiences, but TV still dominates in both the UK and the US.

Some political operations do visuals brilliantly. Perhaps the best people at visuals in the modern political era were the consultants around Ronald Reagan in the 1980s – particularly the *vicar of visuals*, Michael Deaver, and Reagan's regular consultant Roger Ailes, who now heads Fox News. Clearly, Reagan was no amateur himself when it came to TV; he was highly skilled at articulating clear, simple and, yes, emotional messages to popular audiences. But Reagan's team was responsible for some amazing visual imagery.[48]

Reagan's speech at the 40th anniversary of the Normandy landings is a particularly good example of his team's extraordinary feel for emotionally-charged visual imagery. The images of Reagan on the Great Wall of China also spring to mind. Michael Deaver said that he did little for Reagan other than light him well – that was an understatement – but for that alone Deaver should go down as being one of the great modern communications consultants.

Others in politics have also come up with incredibly arresting visuals in recent times. While remembered now for its ill-advised 'Mission Accomplished' banner, President Bush's 2003 arrival at a US aircraft carrier, via a US fighter jet – all lit up in late afternoon orange sunlight like a scene from *Top Gun* – was a truly brilliant piece of TV.[49] Obama's Berlin speech in 2008 in front of a vast German crowd was risky but ultimately extraordinary, as was his 2008 convention speech in a large stadium. Other highlights – and lowlights – from the huge number of political ads over the years are too many to mention.

THE LIMITS OF REASONING

In highlighting the power of emotional arguments, it can appear as if we are arguing that people are not rational *at all* and that they are merely voters to be manipulated by clever campaigns. This is not the intention.

In deciding who to vote for and in forming their opinions on the world, people clearly do go through a process of reasoning of sorts. They match up what they see and hear from campaigns with their own experiences in their jobs and on the high street, and the experiences of their family and friends.[50]

Again, if a political party has been responsible for a major economic downturn where jobs are scarce and prices are high, no amount of clever campaigning is going to persuade people that things are not that bad or that they are the fault of others. People are intelligent.

But in forming views on issues, we have to be realistic about the limits of reasoning and rational argument. Two things are important for us to consider here. Firstly, we know that few people have the time or the inclination to study even the most important political issues in detail. Secondly, we also know that even those that do have the time and inclination for greater study – i.e. academics and expert commentators – still form their views on the basis of emotion.

TIME IS NOT GIVEN TO MAKING RATIONAL DECISIONS

On the first point, logically we know that there is a limit to how much reasoning people can go through on extremely complex issues when they are wrestling with full-time jobs, family commitments, and the inevitable problems that we all have in forming judgements on extremely complicated and new policy issues that arise.[51]

Pollster and political consultant Frank Luntz makes this point in *Words that Work*, arguing it is a "myth" Americans are educated, and the upshot of this "in business and in political communications, is that complexity or intricacy of any degree almost always fails." Luntz goes on to argue it is a myth Americans vote according to candidates' stances on issues: "The reason why issues and ideology are less significant is simply that most Americans don't know the substance behind the issues."[52]

Even on the economy – an issue that directly affects people's wealth – people do not sit down for long periods going through parties' policies on taxation and spending, let alone their plans on technical issues like pension reform or indirect taxation. If people were truly rational, far more would make some sort of attempt to get on top of these issues.

In the area of the economy, people largely make emotionally-driven judgments based on what they hear on TV and what they read about in newspapers – mixed in with what they see and hear in their everyday lives. It can therefore genuinely be better for a political party to have a sympathetic and attractive spokesperson on the economy than an obviously brilliant economist that cannot connect.

THE IRRATIONALITY OF THE INFORMED

On the second point – the emotion that still creeps into the views of the informed – while there has to be a limit to how reasonable and rational voters can be when they are not well informed on key issues, there is evidence to show that many of even the most informed voters hold views formed by emotion rather than reason.

In his book *Expert Political Judgment*, academic Philip E. Tetlock shows many very well-informed professionals make predictions that are driven primarily by their ideological outlook, and when confronted by the visible failure of their predictions they still cling to them, often pointing out that they would have been right but for certain unforeseen circumstances.

Tetlock takes Isaiah Berlin's categorisation of foxes and hedgehogs to show how some people cling to their beliefs whatever the evidence. While foxes embrace complexity – knowing many small things – hedgehogs prefer simplicity and tend only to know "one big thing".[53] Those that know one big thing will be most likely to come up with retrospective explanations for the wisdom of their predictions.

Anyone who regularly reads the political sections of the newspapers or watches political news on TV knows this to be true. The media is full of apparently intelligent pundits making predictions that turn out to be completely wrong, or who praise the apparently clever decision-taking of politicians when no real thought went into it in the first place. Professional pundits like to think of themselves as being objective and rational – and better at analysis and therefore predictions than the average person – but they are as prone to emotional judgments as everybody else.

★★★

Political campaigns understand the central importance of emotion and their general appeals to people are therefore made mostly on an emotional basis, even when the subject matter would imply a colder, more rational approach. There are endless examples of this, even if you only look at the last election cycle in the US.

THE DEVELOPING USES OF EMOTIONAL POWER

This developing research into the power of emotional appeals in politics is starting to change how political organisations operate. In *The Victory Lab,* Sasha Issenberg explains the work of academics Donald Green and Alan Gerber, who have explored how to improve voter turnout (which they also explain in their own book *Get Out the Vote*).[54]

Green and Gerber found, for example, that writing to people telling them that whether they voted was a matter of public record, and their record contrasted negatively with their neighbours', was a powerful way of getting people to vote. Exposing them to feelings of shame – because not voting is perceived to be morally bad – and also showing them that they were out of synch with their neighbours, was a powerful incentive.[55]

These lessons are being taken up by left-leaning campaigns in the US. In some races, where the polls are close but the electorate is very divided on partisan lines, meaning there are few swing voters up for grabs, raising the turnout by mobilising voters whose turnout record is patchy can be the difference between winning and losing.

Given young people and some ethnic minority groups in the US are traditionally under-represented in elections, left-leaning campaigns understand the power of using this sort of emotional pressure to raise overall turnout. Political consultants are now starting to pay attention to the literature being produced by academics in the fields of psychology and behavioural science to move traditionally more difficult to reach voters.

Similarly, the British government has created a *Nudge Unit* that seeks to apply lessons of behavioural science to apparently intractable problems like tax payment rates, smoking, bad diets and so on. This Nudge Unit recently succeeded in improving tax payment rates, for example, by telling people most others in their town had already paid, exposing them to social pressure. The unit is now selling its expertise abroad, having secured a contract with the government of New South Wales in Australia.[56]

THE IMPLICATIONS FOR BUSINESSES

Now that businesses are entering a public conversation about their brand and issues, they must learn to take a similar approach to that taken by campaigns. Many businesses already display a very sophisticated approach to emotional messaging in their advertising and marketing campaigns – the entire concept of branding is, of course, emotional. However, unlike political campaigns, businesses have not managed to transfer these skills into their general public messaging. Many still struggle in public debate.

It is tempting for those that work in corporate communications to think cultivating a more emotional approach is easier for political campaigns, where they deal with subjects passionate people care about. Indeed, it is certainly true to say there are many people that care a great deal about politics and follow it closely. However, as we have seen, campaigns always seek to move people emotionally, even on issues that do not appear to lend themselves to such an approach. Businesses can therefore do far more to develop an emotional approach.

Vast numbers of people really do care about issues like whether the council will grant planning permission for a supermarket, and they care about issues like food safety, the cost of petrol, and about the hiring and firing practices of big companies. And we know that significant minorities of the public care about things like executive salaries, the treatment of suppliers and so on.

Like campaigns, even on issues that are apparently technocratic and boring, businesses can make people feel something. Announcements made about expansion plans can talk about the families given new hope through new jobs; successful years can be talked about in the context of the long history of the firm or the lives and experiences of the successful staff; opposition to new regulations can be blamed on out-of-touch politicians. There is almost always a way for businesses to take bland news stories and give them an emotional tint.

FIVE WAYS BUSINESSES CAN APPLY A MORE EMOTIONAL APPROACH

There are five key ways businesses can apply a more emotional approach to their communications.

1. WILLINGNESS TO TAKE MORE RISKS IN PUBLIC POSITIONING

Businesses should take more risks in their general public positioning and how they inject themselves into public debate. While many businesses prefer to stay out of the media, particularly on issues normally dealt with by their public affairs teams, they actually need to hit the public radar on more issues that move the public emotionally and that define them positively.

For example, while the natural reaction of many firms that face tax rises on their industry is to lobby government directly and keep any row out of the newspapers and away from potentially nervous investors, businesses should at least *consider* the opposite. Sometimes it will benefit a business to have a public row with the government to send a message to customers they are on their side. Sometimes it makes sense to seek out high-profile stories that say something about the business' values and approach.

Businesses do not get many chances to move people in this way and they should take them where they can. Public arguments provoke strong feelings in people. A row along the lines set out above could make people feel sympathy towards the business, or make them feel angry towards the government and make them more likely to follow the story moving forward.

2. LOOKING HARDER FOR NEWSWORTHY STORIES

Related to this, businesses need to re-evaluate what counts as a good story. While businesses always need to explain results, new appointments and general strategy to interested parties through the media, they need to start thinking harder about how to generate coverage that moves people emotionally but stands the chance of being read widely. While the main news bulletins are always going to be beyond the reach of all but the best-known companies, it is still very much a possibility for most businesses to get coverage on popular news sites and blogs, in magazines and on softer news shows.

Some businesses need to consider generating quirkier stories on things like acts of remarkable customer service where a staff member has gone well beyond the call of duty, or highlighting surprising CSR programmes. Some businesses might publicise speeches from senior executives articulating a different and more decent way of conducting operations and treating staff.

3. USE OF EMOTIVE LANGUAGE

Businesses can apply a more emotional approach in the general language they use. Too many businesses send out statements that are too long, too complex, and which use technical or insider's language. Businesses often behave as if the media outlet they are providing a statement for is itself the audience, rather than being the intermediary to the audiences outside in the real world. Businesses need to develop a more people-friendly approach to their communications and above all use language that moves people emotionally.

Their (hopefully extensive) opinion research will point the way, but they should be more willing to deploy concepts like fairness, decency, aspiration, hope, concern, and even fear or fun. They need constantly to think about what will attract the attention of ordinary people who come across their stories and read their comments. If they could not imagine someone nodding in agreement and potentially repeating their statement, they should think again about it.

4. BETTER VISUALS

Establishing effective visuals is undoubtedly difficult, particularly from an earned media perspective when the organisation is effectively collaborating with a media organisation to create the right shots. But much of the hard work is done by thinking about what it is that the organisation actually wants to project – the logistics follow on from this.

Some people reading this might think they have a more fundamental problem – their organisation is not high-profile enough to get on TV and not rich enough to buy significant ad space. There is no doubt that if you work in government or a high-profile campaign, getting on TV is relatively easy. The bottom line remains true though – if you accept visual imagery is extremely powerful, then it is worth thinking hard about how to create visuals in principle.

Perhaps there are opportunities to develop visual material to sit on the business' website or social media platforms. Perhaps short ads can be made relatively cheaply to be placed on relevant websites and social media platforms. Perhaps it is worth thinking hard about the right backdrops to those events that are likely to get coverage – announcements of results, for example. Businesses should certainly not think that visuals are not worth worrying about if they are not being called up regularly by the main news programmes. Visuals are always worth worrying about.

5. TAKING A MORAL STANCE

Businesses need to develop a more self-conscious *moral* approach to their communications. Of all of these methods, this might seem the most difficult for businesses to achieve. Can they really take a moral approach as profit-making corporate brands? Emphatically, yes. Businesses can show that they have a strong moral outlook, that they are honest, decent and trustworthy. This is what many firms are doing already with their CSR campaigns, but they can take this approach into their wider, public communications.

Part of this response will be similar to the emotional response. In other words, businesses can simply be more active in playing moral arguments into their communications and using language which stresses issues like fairness, decency and so on. Similarly, they can also choose to create what you might call *moral moments* – interesting events designed to secure public and media attention and which tell a moral story. Again, much of this might come out of the business' CSR programme, but it might also include highlighting their enlightened working practices, generous compensation of customers for poor service or sponsorship of worthy events.

Businesses should also get into the habit of mobilising third parties on their behalf, getting respected people to engage for them. People will always trust a business' position on a set of issues more if independent and respected people come out and back them, or say the same things publicly. This is time consuming and difficult but the rewards can be massive. I will deal with this in more detail in the next chapter.

Crucially, however, businesses will only be able to take the moral high ground if they really believe they have a right to it. In other words, it is partly psychological. In my experience, while many businesses will say behind closed doors they are right and their opponents wrong, they feel nervous about saying this publicly. Sometimes you get the sense that they feel guilty about, for example, disagreeing with morally confident politicians, trade unions or NGOs, while at other times you feel that they do not believe the public would ever come down on their side.

George Eustice, previously the spokesman for David Cameron in opposition, and now a Conservative MP for Camborne and Redruth in Cornwall, picks up on this nervousness:

> "When it comes to public opinion, perceived motives count for a lot, so moral arguments frequently trump factual or technical arguments. Political parties instinctively understand this and a desire to seize the moral high ground sits easily with the passion of political ideas. However, very few corporations are capable of doing the same. They lack sufficiently robust organisation

structures to deliver themselves through the pain barrier along the way to the moral high ground and their institutional cultures make them prone to being snivelling, apologetic and defensive instead."[57]

Eustice has a point. Many businesses do find moral confidence uncomfortable and many of their communications campaigns suffer as a result. But, assuming that they *are* right on an issue, businesses should be extremely confident in their public communications and should explicitly seek to take the moral high ground with no feelings of self-consciousness whatever. As we will see, endorsements always help, but the public are sensible and will sympathise with whoever has the best arguments.

Businesses do sometimes get this right. A good example of a corporate campaign that tapped into moral arguments was the Greggs-led campaign against the *pasty tax* in the Budget of 2012. Working with sympathetic media outlets, Greggs and other bakeries argued that an additional tax on hot takeaway food would unfairly hit working class customers. Speaking at a protest event outside Downing Street, the Greggs Chief Executive Ken McMeikan said the government was "out of touch with the poorest people in this country who need aspirations and hopes – not higher taxes."[58]

This campaign ended up providing additional contrast between the actions of the government's senior politicians – some of them coming from extremely wealthy families – and the people they were supposed to be helping out in a recession. It took on real moral significance and it was no surprise when the government decided to back down.

Another example comes from McDonald's, who made a great deal of their apprenticeships programme in the UK in the latter stages of Labour's time in power. Thought of unfairly by some as being a provider of low-skill jobs with few opportunities – *McJobs* – the fast food retailer made huge efforts to show that it was providing meaningful careers to huge numbers of young people in the UK.

McDonald's obviously takes staff development seriously but, whether it was the intention or not, it tapped into widespread public and political concern about the opportunities available for young people in the UK. They began to take the moral high ground at an important time for the firm and were able to make it clear that while others merely talked about the problem of youth unemployment and poor opportunities, they were actually doing something about it.[59]

These sorts of morally confident campaigns are, however, a rarity. Businesses need to put away their natural tendency to hedge, and also the occasional tendency to cede too much moral respect to opposition groups, and command the moral high ground.

GENERAL RULES FOR MESSAGING

Businesses, like political campaigns, should remember the power of emotion and morality in their communications. Their public-facing materials – everything from newspaper columns, to their blogs, to their public statements – should keep this in mind. But there are other characteristics of successful messaging that businesses should reflect.

Journalists and consultants have written a great deal about this over the years, with many suggestions for the defining characteristics of successful messaging. In *Words that Work*, Frank Luntz writes about 'The Ten Rules of Effective Language', which includes advice such as using small words and small sentences, being consistent, speaking aspirationally and bringing language to life through visualisation.[60]

Journalist Joe Klein argues that politicians should at all times seek "authenticity", being as real and unvarnished as possible to engage voters[61] and veteran Republican consultant Joseph Gaylord warns politicians, in his excellent *Flying Upside Down*, against focusing on obvious public priorities, arguing that it is hard to be distinctive and credible in these areas.[62] All of these provide extremely useful food for thought.

Having worked for a number of years in political campaigns, in the commercial world for major brands and also in government, I have established my own list. For me, messages must be:

1. Clear

2. Targeted

3. Credible

4. Interesting

5. Dynamic

These are the issues that have been on my mind as the campaigns I have worked on have taken shape. We will explore these characteristics in turn now.

1. CLEAR

Messages must be clear. That means they must be easily understandable for any reasonably educated person – requiring no additional explanation – and they must be simple. This is so obvious that it ought to require little further comment. But a lot of organisations, despite knowing they need to create clear messages, still end up putting out messages to public audiences that are excessively complex, on issues most people know nothing about, or that are just badly written.

Businesses struggle with clarity for a number of reasons. Firstly, and this is most common with statements created ahead of their own campaigns or launches, they find it difficult to stress priorities. As with strategy making, they feel as if stressing some issues and not others sends the message that they are saying certain things are not important. They therefore have a tendency to put too much into their messages.

Another problem tends to be the assumption of much greater knowledge amongst public audiences than is realistic, and the use of technical and obscure language. A related problem is many businesses argue the material they are dealing with is more complex than that in political campaigns, suggesting political consultants who try to help them are being naïve and messages cannot be made as clear as they would like.

I have never had any sympathy at all for businesses that make these sorts of excuses about why they cannot create clear messages. The only answer here would be, "OK, let's just accept that this is too hard and put out unclear messages." This is not an option if a firm wants to communicate effectively.

Messages on virtually any subject can always be made simple and clear with serious thought. Think about the sorts of issues that campaigns deal with – think about the banking crisis, general macroeconomic policy, the Middle East, public service reform and financing. The list of extremely complex subject matter is endless but political campaigns get through with a mix of willpower and polling.

Paul Begala, one of Bill Clinton's consultants in his successful 1992 campaign, explained this better than anyone. Just ahead of Clinton's first major presidential debate, Begala was trying to get Clinton to really focus on the clarity of his message, which Clinton was complaining was really hard.

At this point, Begala pulled out a copy of the New Testament and, giving it to Clinton, asked him to read aloud a section from St John's Gospel. While Begala set his stopwatch, Clinton read out these lines: "For God so loved the world He gave His only begotten son so that whoever believes in Him shall not die but have everlasting life." When Clinton finished Begala said, "Governor, if the Lord God can explain all the important tenets of Christianity in 6.7 seconds, surely you can tell us if you're for the balanced budget amendment."[63]

2. TARGETED

Messages must be targeted. I will not repeat the arguments of the last chapter, but we know businesses must think hard about who their messages are designed to move, and create and deliver them accordingly. The last chapter showed how the concept of micro targeting has become commonplace within political campaigns.

Campaigns have been able to fuse vast amounts of consumer data available on voters' behaviour with polling data and use this information – with the opportunities for cheap and accurate delivery provided by the growth of the internet – to reach very specific groups of people. You now hear stories of campaigns buying up very small amounts of ad space in local communities in order to plant specific messages that are highly likely to appeal to a small number of people living there.

3. CREDIBLE

Credibility is important. For messages to have traction with the media and outside world, they must pass the reality test. For example, if your candidate in a political campaign is extremely rich, it is obviously relatively more difficult to talk about the struggles of life for the poorest. Not impossible, but more difficult.

This was clearly on the minds of the Mitt Romney campaign in 2012 – how do you engage middle-class voters on the economy when you are rich and they are struggling in the downturn? Having focused primarily on the macro economy at first, talking about how his record as a successful corporate executive meant that he could successfully manage the US economy, Governor Romney moved towards a message of helping to grow the middle class. He carried this off reasonably well in the first presidential debate, but it was evidently a difficult pitch.

When they engage in public debate, businesses need to have this credibility point in mind. Businesses need to ask themselves whether or not it is credible for them to be pushing a particular message given their background, their record, their perceived strategy and self-interest, and the image of their senior executives.

It would not be credible for a retailer looking to establish a new supermarket in a local town full of independent shops to claim that their new store would improve the quality of food available. Better for that supermarket would be to talk about cheaper food, or providing more family-friendly shopping.

Similarly, it would not be credible for a fast food retailer looking to avoid further regulation on its industry to argue that its primary objective was to provide nutritious food for the masses. It is better for them to point out that more regulation cuts into profits and therefore their ability to offer jobs in a downturn.

4. INTERESTING

Messages must be interesting. This falls into that category of being apparently excessively obvious. But, again, many organisations still create messages for the media and public audiences that are uninteresting to everybody except themselves and a small number of sector specialists. I have been in messaging sessions where businesses have wanted to agree messages which would never, ever make it into a mainstream newspaper and which nobody in the outside world would ever listen to or repeat. In fact, these messages would even bore them at weekends when they were not in the office.

Organisations must see themselves as others do. Occasionally, this is difficult, but it is always possible to make messages more interesting than they might be. The British pub industry has managed this to good effect over the last decade, pointing out, for example, the number of pubs that have been closing each week as a result of the smoking ban and increased regulation. This is one of those messages that could have been boring – many pubs are struggling – to one which is endlessly repeated in the media and which you occasionally hear people repeating in ordinary life.

5. DYNAMIC

Finally, messages need to be dynamic. This means organisations must be careful the messages they create cannot be neutralised by their opposition in a simple countermove, or do not become stale because they are of limited interest or designed for the very short term. This is one of the most difficult things for campaigns and businesses to get right, but it is extremely important that they try to achieve this.

For example, imagine a firm is trying to create a campaign to persuade the government against banning the advertising of a particular product. A trade association for the sector in question might say that legislation could never work. That message may work perfectly well but what happens if the government trails a plan for how the legislation would work in practice and the advertising regulators respond by backing it? Clearly, this is always a danger in any communications operation.

Campaigns and businesses can minimise the chances of being blown out of the water by thinking hard about dynamic messaging. The trade association could develop messaging around the growing movement against the plans – and then start to mobilise third parties against it. Or it could develop messaging around how the real target for government should be in a different piece of legislation, and then show endless examples of how not going after the real target is the problem. These campaigns could not be shut down in one move by government and would have the chance to create momentum.

Political campaigns have an instinctive feel for creating campaigns with the potential to go somewhere. They do not base messages on things that can be neutralised by their opposition simply saying, "we agree", and they do not create messages that will be out of date in a week because the event they were focusing on has come and gone.

Campaigns ask themselves how far the opposition is likely to be able to go in compromising before they lose their core support or before they look inconsistent and unprincipled. You often hear political campaigns say that their opposition has "nowhere to go" or that they have been "boxed in". Businesses need to develop this same instinctive sense for dynamism.

CHAPTER FIVE
GENERATING ENDORSEMENTS

ENDORSEMENTS IN CAMPAIGNS

POLITICAL CAMPAIGNS AND movements have been generating endorsements from third parties for decades. They are so ubiquitous in American politics, Chris Cillizza, the *Washington Post* journalist who blogs as The Fix, created the tongue-in-cheek but insightful *endorsement hierarchy*.

At the bottom he puts the *pariah endorsement* – the one from someone a campaign does not actually want. At the top he puts the *symbolic endorsement* – one he describes as "a passing of the torch, a healing of an old wound, or a laying on of hands". He puts the late Senator Ted Kennedy's endorsement of Barack Obama in early 2008 in this category.[64]

For all Chris Cillizza's *seen it all before* narrative, endorsements still make news, even when expected. In the 2012 election cycle, despite the fact the US Chamber of Commerce had been running ads backing Republican candidates, their formal endorsements still made news. Unions endorsing Democrats also made news. There are few things a campaign can do that generate simple good news – endorsements are one.

Endorsements from the right sorts of people say something powerful about a candidate or campaign that cannot be generated from the campaign itself. A politician can talk about his or her virtues and record with some effect, but this message is obviously more powerful if the words come out of someone else's mouth. Independent voices are always trusted more than direct participants in a debate.

Chris LaCivita is one of America's best and most respected campaign consultants and has specialised in the field of third-party campaigns and endorsements. A decorated former US Marine, he was the chief strategist for the Swift Boat Veterans for Truth campaign that derailed Senator John Kerry's presidential campaign in 2004. LaCivita told me the case for endorsements is obvious:

> "Nothing is worse than a politician on TV talking about how great they are, which is why so many campaigns find other people and organizations to speak *for* them. Nothing brings home a point more than 'someone like me'."[65]

If the people making endorsements are associated with a particular set of values or virtues, this shapes the candidate or campaign's preferred image or underlines their commitment to a particular set of priorities. For example, a candidate keen to show they are honest might welcome an endorsement from groups of religious preachers or clergy. A candidate seeking to look tough on crime might welcome endorsements from former senior police officers or groups representing victims of crime.

Endorsements can help a campaign make progress with certain parts of the electorate that had been sceptical. If a campaign had problems being heard by a particular group of workers, or people in a particular area, an endorsement by someone trusted by these hard-to-reach groups creates more sympathy (remember Munzenberg?). You see this regularly in the US, where presidential candidates welcome endorsements from well-known people from particular minorities, or by fellow politicians from swing states.

An endorsement from a particular group can make attacks from that same group less credible. If a candidate was worried senior executives from a given industry were going to attack their economic policy, endorsements from a small number within the same industry in advance would allow the candidate to claim opinion was divided and they had support. Generating even small numbers of supporters can act as a spoiler to the opponent's planned use of endorsements.

While this is most important for issues-focused campaigns, endorsements can change the balance of power in a debate for all campaigns. A campaign perceived to have little support publicly can use endorsements to show it actually has widespread support. Campaigns once ignored by politicians and the media can *force* people to take them seriously. This might come from a handful of high-profile endorsements or from the mobilisation of large numbers of ordinary people, but there is nothing like public validation to change the balance of power within a debate.

This crucial shift is not just that people can see large numbers of others agree with a campaign on an issue – it is psychological too. People are less likely to criticise a campaign if they think it will put them on the wrong side of public opinion. Most prefer to feel in touch with opinion. Organisations that generate endorsements are not only potentially turning a debate on its head, but they are establishing the equivalent of a force field around them, making attacks less likely and less powerful than they would otherwise be.

THE BRITISH ANTI-EURO CAMPAIGN

One of the best endorsement operations of recent times was run in Britain, during the extremely heated debate on whether Britain should enter the euro – one of the highest profile debates for a decade. The No campaign, formed in 2000, was a business-led coalition against British entry that would have formed the official opposition had the government called a referendum at some point between 2000 and 2003. I joined the campaign in 2000.

The campaign was important for two reasons. Firstly, at the end of the 1990s, the Conservative Party had been wiped out electorally and remained very unpopular across the country. Opposition to the euro depended on securing the support of large numbers of non-Tories. Creating a new, independent campaign allowed this. People turned off by a Conservative spokesperson would listen to a corporate executive, economist or academic.

Secondly, the polls were clear. The campaign's detailed research showed the public opposed the euro by two to one. More delving showed the public was split into three reasonably equally sized groups. A third of the population were completely opposed to the euro. They would pull Britain out of the EU altogether. Another third were committed to the euro. There was then a crucial middle third of people who were vaguely opposed to the euro as the debate stood, but were persuadable. They were worried above all about the effects of euro entry on their jobs and financial security (as later events proved, rightly).

The No campaign focused overwhelmingly on this middle third by mobilising vast numbers of credible businesspeople and academics to argue joining the euro would damage the economy and cost jobs. Typically, this saw the campaign's research and media operation generate negative stories on the euro, and use businesspeople to comment on the stories in the press and in broadcast media to ram the message home. While the pro-euro Britain in Europe campaign tried constantly to link its opponents with the unpopular Conservative Party, it never succeeded because of the scale of the endorsement operation of the No campaign.

While the No campaign initially struggled to secure the endorsement of a relatively small number of businesspeople – those who signed public letters opposing the euro and who joined the Business Council of public supporters – the campaign worked tirelessly to grow its list.

By the autumn of 2000 the No campaign was able to showcase hundreds of businesspeople hostile to the euro in a double-page ad in the *Financial Times*. Another ad signed by even more businesspeople was displayed in *The Times* a year later. By 2003, ahead of the government's announcement that Britain would not be entering the euro, the campaign was able to deploy on the broadcast media the chief executives of some of Britain's biggest firms – as well as small business owners on the Welsh coast – at almost no notice.

George Eustice was in charge of the No campaign's regional efforts before becoming campaign director in 2002. Eustice argues that the No campaign's success was in large part down to its ability to line up large numbers of people behind a single message:

> "Herd instinct drives the tone and nature of media coverage on most issues, so projecting a uniform pattern of information, where possible, is important. That is why endorsements matter. In the case of the euro debate, in the early stages, the prevailing assumption among both the public and the media was that business wanted the euro, so feeding dissonance into the bloodstream of debate neutralised the pro euro campaign's advantage."[66]

The government ultimately decided to back away from the euro in 2003. The No campaign's near-perfect endorsement strategy was undoubtedly a deciding factor.

OTHER BRITISH ENDORSEMENT CAMPAIGNS

I have been involved in a number of other successful endorsement operations in the UK that highlight the power of this approach. In 2004 I was part of a team that mobilised 500 senior NHS doctors to call for a change in the way the NHS operates.

The campaign – Doctors for Reform, run by Nick Herbert and Andrew Haldenby's influential Reform think tank – not only secured a front-page story in *The Times* when it was launched, but managed to place significant numbers of articulate doctors across national and local media to make the case for change. While it was difficult for supporters of the euro to hit out effectively against businesspeople in the euro debate, it was even harder for opponents of change in the healthcare sector to argue effectively against brilliant doctors.

Later in 2004, I managed the North East Says No campaign (against the introduction of a Regional Assembly in the area). As with the anti-euro campaign, North East Says No was an endorsement machine with an aggressive and effective media campaign attached. The team, led by brilliant local businessman Phil Cummings, recruited large numbers of senior businesspeople across the region to frame the debate as local businesspeople against out of touch politicians. The media team then mobilised these businesspeople into the media to make their case to the public.

Looking back, it is easy to see these campaigns as having been *inevitably* successful. When they are described like this, it all sounds obvious and straightforward. But, as indicated earlier, endorsement operations are extremely time consuming and hard to pull off. Mobilising large numbers of high-profile independent people, often with full-time jobs, is a logistical nightmare and takes serious time and effort.

Henry de Zoete, now a government special adviser, but who formerly specialised in third-party campaigns, says:

> "Surprisingly few comms agencies really focus on the endorsement business. That might come down to a lack of imagination for some or doubts that these endorsements count for much in the media, but it's maybe also a reflection on the fact that endorsements just take so much effort to secure. The letters that you see signed by even a small number of independent voices will have taken a determined team weeks to get. The pay off is worth it but no one should be under any illusion that these things are easy or quick to make happen."[67]

The pay-off can be huge. The No campaign changed the way the media and the public thought about corporate attitudes to the single currency. Once it was conventional wisdom to assume that the corporate world wanted to join the euro, but soon it was accepted that business was divided or even hostile. Similarly the Doctors for Reform campaign injected real shock into the system back in 2003, showing that large numbers of senior doctors were sceptical about the NHS continuing to operate in its current form.

THE NEED FOR CORPORATE ENDORSEMENTS

Now that ordinary people take a lead role in determining the reputation of businesses in public debate, businesses should be developing expertise in the field of endorsements as a matter of priority. Like political campaigns, they need to accept that influencing the public partly depends on deploying credible and trusted spokespeople in the form of independent voices. According to Henry de Zoete:

> "The media and the general public are understandably more likely to believe what outside experts or ordinary people say – in fact, pretty much all independent voices – than what politicians and party workers say. The same is true in business. A CEO can say what he likes but a trusted outside expert in the same field, even if they're actually less qualified, is trusted much more, just as a consumer or a group of consumers are more trusted."[68]

This point about trust is important. The global PR giant Edelman produces an annual report on the issue of trust – the Edelman Trust Barometer. In 2012 they asked people in 20 countries how credible a piece of information on a company would be if it came from various different sources. Most trusted was an "academic or expert", followed by a "technical expert in the company" and "a person like yourself". The CEO was the second bottom, just above "government official or regulator".[69]

Businesses should see the generation of endorsements as a way to deal defensively with the rise of opinion, and also positively to define their brand and key issues. The rise of opinion and the explosion of the internet provides businesses with the ability not only to market key endorsements from individuals, but also to recruit and mobilise large numbers of ordinary members of the public in campaigns. A small number of businesses have followed this approach, but far more businesses will do so in the future.

A combination of social media and general online advocacy, combined with mainstream media, can help businesses generate campaigns supported by tens of thousands of people. New and simple online tools help businesses mobilise those people to send emails and letters to decision makers, sign petitions, make calls, and recruit their friends. Social media platforms also make it easier to target advertising at just the right sort of people who would be interested in a particular campaign – and also to target advertising at those decision takers and key influencers that the campaign needs to reach.

WHAT MAKES ENDORSEMENTS WORK

We have looked at how endorsements work – we know what success looks like – but how should firms actually approach the generation of endorsements in the first place? What characteristics does an endorsement programme need to have, if it wants to be successful?

Most obviously, the message the independent voices express needs to be powerful. Occasionally the quality of the endorsements will be so high what the people say is irrelevant. For example, if an organisation is lucky enough to be able to unveil the endorsement of *the* celebrity of the moment or a handful of well-known figures the public really respect, simple association might be enough to make people look more favourably on the organisation.

However, this is rare and, as a rule, endorsements only really work when a serious message is attached. It might be good for a campaign to have the support of a popular former politician or senior corporate executive, but the endorsement carries more weight if he or she says something substantial. That might be issues-based (endorsing a policy decision) or values-based (endorsing a quality or characteristic), but it needs to be clear and powerful.

The independent voices themselves should be as high quality and interesting as possible. Sometimes celebrities help but often it is better to use independent voices that stand for something because of the role they play in society, for example if they are community leaders or well-known employers.

The number of endorsements should also be significant. While sometimes a single person will be so respected they make news, usually organisations need to mobilise a significant number. Journalists have no understanding of the effort required to secure even small numbers of endorsements.

Getting a dozen Chief Executives to sign a letter on a relatively straightforward policy can take days and getting scores to sign a letter or ad can take weeks. The fact journalists do not understand the process underlines the point that campaigns have to mobilise significant amounts of people to get cut-through. There are times when the media is so desperate to stack up a story that they will take even a small number to illustrate *a growing trend*, but this is rare.

It is perfectly possible to mobilise significant numbers of ordinary people if together they tell a story. A political campaign trying to get traction in a particular part of the country where they are under-represented might mobilise significant numbers of small and medium-sized firms from that area, showing that ordinary, local employers are throwing their weight behind a campaign. Similarly, it might be that a significant number of public sector workers sends a strong message.

OVERCOMING THE CONCERNS OF BUSINESSES

American and British businesses – American ones to a much greater extent – have taken steps to apply some of these lessons. However, despite some progress, businesses tend to be reluctant to take this approach. From my own experience, I know how businesses normally very confident in the field of media relations suddenly lose their nerve when it comes to dealing with endorsements from people they do not know and therefore do not trust.

Some worry mobilising third parties would in principle see them lose control over their brand. They worry they would be creating, in effect, large numbers of brand ambassadors that might end up embarrassing the firm by saying all sorts of things they do not agree with. Depending on the issue, they also worry some of the people that might be drawn to an endorsement operation might not be the sorts of people they would want to be associated with.

Other businesses worry mobilising public voices behind an issues-based campaign designed to influence the government would anger the politicians. They fear it would raise the stakes too much. This is often partly a reflection of their concern that people they recruit and unleash might express themselves much more aggressively than they would do themselves as a business.

These concerns are understandable but misplaced. While businesses can and should provide guidance to the public voices they seek to mobilise, if the campaign is constructed in the right way, no politician or media outlet is going to think that those people backing their cause are in some way owned by the business. That is not to say careful handling is not required, but campaigns should not go wrong if managed by competent people.

Whenever I have constructed grassroots campaigns for businesses that have mobilised ordinary people I have always taken steps to keep the client in control of their own brand. For example, I never create a situation where people become *members* of a client's campaign and I tend to advise clients to create independent identities for the campaign, with the client's name as a visible but secondary identity. People are therefore joining a *cause* that the business happens to be leading.

Furthermore, I always advise clients to be extremely clear about what their campaign stands for, to prevent any sub-campaigns developing.

The same principles apply in mobilising elite endorsements – it works best when people back a *cause*.

In any case, businesses need to remember most people genuinely are decent, reasonable and conduct themselves in the right way. There will always be some who take things too far – particularly on social media platforms – but generally people can be trusted. At heart, businesses know this – they just need to be reminded that the sorts of people they are seeking to mobilise are often simply their customers in another setting.

On their second concern, businesses have to accept that politicians and their advisers respond to pressure. Full stop. Their lives are so chaotic and their obsession with positive coverage so strong, pressure invariably works best. Politicians will not hold a grudge against a business they think is supported by the public. They will simply flip their position to agree with the business in question and probably convince themselves they agreed all along.

That said, the endorsement game is rougher than traditional media relations and public affairs. The power of third-party endorsements in politics and the corporate world causes a reaction in the media and from the groups being targeted. Also, while people can be trusted to behave decently, there is no question that outsiders, and particularly the public, express themselves more directly and with less nuance than insiders working for a company. These are all *good things,* and businesses need to relax and make the jump.

HOW BUSINESSES ARE GETTING INTO ENDORSEMENTS

Some businesses in both Britain and the US *have* taken steps in the right direction in the endorsement game and all businesses should learn from them. The types of campaign have varied – some have developed coalitions with other businesses to push particular issues, while others have mobilised members of the public behind an issue-based campaign. A few firms have also tried to play in well-known individuals in the same way that political campaigns use them. Here are some examples.

THE BRITISH DRINKS INDUSTRY

In 2007 the British drinks industry launched a major campaign to deal with the growing prospect of new government regulations to deal with problem drinking. For some time, the media had been full of stories about how "binge drinking" had increased and was undermining the health of the country and leading to a surge in anti-social behaviour. At a time when the government was developing its alcohol strategy, this put the industry in a vulnerable position.

To combat this, the Wine and Spirit Trade Association, under their extremely competent former Chief Executive Jeremy Beadles, not only changed its language to become more public-oriented – focusing on the impact of, for example, higher taxes on the price of people's drinks – but they also launched the Responsible Drinkers Alliance, which mobilised large numbers of ordinary people across the country behind a less regulatory approach.[70]

The British Beer & Pub Association launched a similar public-facing campaign shortly after, to mobilise the public against measures that would harm the British pub. Their Save the Pub campaign secured widespread support in the media. All of this undoubtedly changed the overall terms of the debate on alcohol in the UK, turning the debate on its head and showing politicians unambiguously the public was opposed to higher taxes and higher prices on their drinks.

PORSCHE

In 2008, German luxury carmaker Porsche launched a major public campaign against the then Mayor of London's proposed introduction of a new £25 daily charge on higher carbon dioxide-emitting vehicles. This included a major campaign in the media, securing significant amounts of positive coverage and mobilising large numbers of ordinary people via a campaign website to sign a petition against the charge and make their voices heard publicly.[71]

The campaign turned what had been seen as a positive issue for the mayor – which few had dared to campaign against – to being one that was seen as a net negative. In the end, a newly elected mayor refused to introduce the charge.

YES TO HIGH SPEED RAIL

In 2011, a small group of businesspeople led by Westbourne's James Bethell (who really gets the endorsement game) and the *Transport Times'* David Begg, came together to support government plans to develop HS2 – the high-speed train line linking London with the Midlands and the North of England. The debate, which had previously been dominated by hostile groups in the rural Midlands, was significantly changed by the mobilisation of large numbers of executives from the Midlands and North.[72]

The campaign began with a letter signed by significant numbers of businesspeople in the *Financial Times,* and then played these businesspeople into the media debate, also creating a website to inform the public of the benefits of the plans and to recruit their support. Again, the debate was turned on its head, with the media now seeing that the proposed development had significant support.

TERMINATE THE RATE

A successful campaign was created and run by BT and mobile network 3 from May 2009, when they successfully mobilised over 150,000 people to sign a petition calling on the government to reduce mobile *termination rates.* They also secured the support of, for example, the GMB union and the Federation of Small Businesses. Ultimately, telecoms regulator Ofcom did decide to take steps to lower these rates.[73]

ANTI-CONGESTION CHARGE CAMPAIGN

In 2008, a group of businesses based in Manchester came together to campaign against the proposed introduction of a new congestion charge in the city. The campaign saw the people of Manchester overwhelmingly oppose the charge in a referendum, not only making it extremely unlikely that a new charge will be introduced there, but less likely other cities will come up with their own plans.[74]

★★★

These are some of the main British examples, but campaigns are more common in the US.

EXAMPLES FROM THE US

NEW YORKERS FOR BEVERAGE CHOICES

As we have already seen, in 2012, various soft drinks firms came together to create a major campaign against New York Mayor Michael Bloomberg and the Board of Health's support for a ban on large sugar-sweetened drinks being sold in restaurants and various other places.

The campaign, New Yorkers for Beverage Choices, was backed by a huge number of outlets in the city and collected the support of over half a million people online.[75] The website encourages people to write to their council members opposing the ban, which it makes a very simple process. The campaign focused hard on the issue of personal choice and is still mobilising opposition to the move. It is unclear ultimately where this will all end.

THE CAMPAIGN TO CUT CREDIT CARD TRANSACTION FEES

In 2009, a group of representatives from the retail sector got together to campaign against the fees imposed on credit card transactions by credit card companies, who pass the fees on to banks. The fees amounted to 44 cents per transaction, or $16bn a year, and fell directly on the retail sector.

The campaign that the retailers put together – which ended up persuading lawmakers in congress to cap the fees in a Senate vote – mobilised vast numbers of small retailers to lobby their Senators. They also flew large numbers of retailers to Washington to meet with their representatives directly, held press events and pushed a strong media campaign. One of Washington's main political journals *The Hill* named this campaign the lobbying victory of the year in December 2011.[76]

WORKING FAMILIES FOR WAL-MART

Back in 2005, the retailer Wal-Mart created a new campaign – Working Families for Wal-Mart – mobilising ordinary people and businesses to advocate on their behalf to bring balance to a public debate dominated by hostile voices. Wal-Mart also created a *war room* to monitor the debate around their firm and to direct responses. While Wal-Mart have come in for criticism for their campaign approach – with accusations of the secret use of PR firms – they have managed to develop something of a human face to their operation. Those people that have criticised them most loudly would probably have done so regardless of Wal-Mart's approach.[77]

ENERGY WORKS

In a move to try to educate the public about the industry, the American Petroleum Institute, which represents hundreds of American energy firms, launched a campaign in 2012 called Energy Works. The campaign's website features videos of workers talking about the industry which, as Wal-Mart's campaign tried to do, put a human face on an industry often accused of caring only about profit. The website also encourages people to sign up to take action to protect and promote the industry.[78]

THE FUTURE OF ENDORSEMENTS

Businesses have lost much of the control they could once expect to assert over their own reputation and key issues. Reputation management is now a much more collaborative process – the result of a public dialogue between the firm, interested parties and ordinary members of the public. The traditional skills of advertising, marketing and media relations remain relevant, but skills in public dialogue are going to become increasingly important.

Mitt Romney might have been right when he famously said in the 2012 presidential campaign that corporations are people too – in the sense that businesses are employers and often significant parts of the local community, and who should be confident about engaging in public debate and defending their record – but this is all relative.

Businesses will always be in a stronger position to defend their record and campaign positively if they have sympathetic voices backing them up. The motives of corporations will always be questioned in public debate – many people, even those who read pro-capitalist, right-leaning newspapers, can occasionally worry about the motives and behaviour of the corporate world.

While it will be different for every firm, businesses should throw themselves into the endorsements game. For some, that might mean mobilising public voices on a large scale to make gains on a particular issue. For others it might mean working collaboratively on issues with businesses in the same field. Some businesses might engage with respected third-party organisations or well-known individuals on various projects simply to associate with respected people. Businesses will judge what is right for them specifically, but all must engage.

In constructing such campaigns, businesses need to have a clear objective and strategy and know exactly what they want their endorsements to achieve. This will guide their choice of people to approach and help them decide on the look and feel of the campaign.

CHAPTER SIX
TAKING THE RIGHT DECISIONS

THE HIDDEN SKILL OF DECISION-TAKING

"CAMPAIGNS ARE ABOUT managing chaos – and chaos lives in indecision. Campaign organizations are built around making important decisions, not once a day but once an hour. A clear chain of command and confident decision-making are as important as the message itself. Successful campaigns are built on these organizational designs."[79]

So says Chris LaCivita, the Republican consultant who not only made Swift Boat Veterans for Truth such a big success, but who has worked and consulted on a vast number of successful campaigns across the US. Opponents who face LaCivita's campaigns know they are going to be disciplined, ruthlessly focused and action-oriented. He famously managed George Allen's hard-fought campaign in 2000 to beat Democrat incumbent Senator Chuck Robb, a campaign that won *PR Week's* campaign of the year.

Every political consultant knows how right these words from Chris LaCivita are. They know effective campaign action is dependent on an organisation taking the right decisions in the first place. People can only be moved if they actually receive emails, leaflets and phone calls, and if they see an organisation's case online and see its ads. Despite its unglamorous nature, organisational design and effective decision-taking are absolutely vital parts of effective campaigning.

Many of us have worked in dysfunctional political campaigns where unclear reporting lines and excessive bureaucracy made decision-taking impossible. Occasionally, this is down to the dynamic between the most senior staff. Usually, however, it is down to politicians refusing to take decisions themselves and refusing to create a structure that allows decisions to be taken for them. In such circumstances, even the best campaign staff can find themselves kicking their heels waiting for direction from above, or having to return to decisions they had already taken because the politician could not agree on action.

Behind a high proportion of internal coups and senior level resignations in campaign life, there is a story of internal frustration with the decision-taking capability of the campaign. And when consultants talk with each other about how their respective campaigns are going, they almost always dwell on the speed at which decisions are taken and the nature of internal bureaucracy.

The fact is, organisational design is really hard and even the highest-profile and best-funded campaigns struggle to get this right. Picking just one example, in 2008 Hillary Clinton's ultimately unsuccessful campaign in the Democratic primaries was said to be marred by internal disagreements between top advisers.

As Samuel L. Popkin, the academic and campaign consultant, describes in his book *The Candidate*, "There was so much conflict [in Hillary Clinton's campaign] about where one staffer's lane ended and another's began – not to mention their profits and status as campaign professionals – that the interservice rivalry choked off cooperation and innovation."[80]

While there are plenty of examples of organisational dysfunction in campaigns, businesses should still look to political campaigns for guidance on organisational design because where they do work they are classic models of high-functioning decision-taking under intense pressure. Corporate literature often rightly turns to the military to learn lessons in decision-taking; as we will see later, there have been some brilliant theorists in the military on the concepts of organisational design and strategy. But campaigns generate some hugely impressive operations too, in an area more directly applicable to corporate communications.

THE WAR ROOM

Any campaign needs an effective decision-taking capability. Staff always need leadership and direction, and this is particularly important in political campaigns where the chaos of daily events, the intense time pressure and the activities of the other side all demand the right decisions are taken quickly, day after day. This has become even more important in recent times as the complexity of campaign operations grows. These days, the biggest campaigns are run on the scale of large companies, with massive budgets and huge numbers of staff across multiple sites.

Regardless of the scale of the political operation, the overall challenges are the same: in a time of uncertainty or even chaos, how to take the right decisions fast and adapt to changing circumstances to maintain a focus on public influence. Speed and adaptability are everything. Since the early 1990s, campaigns have been using the *war room* concept to meet these challenges.

The war room is part physical space, part state of mind. It is ultimately the place where key decisions are taken on the direction of the campaign, from a medium to long-term strategic perspective and from a day-to-day operational perspective. The war room works by collecting together in one place the key decision-takers in the campaign – staff who bring with them broad and up-to-date knowledge on what is going on in their areas and the authority to take decisions in their areas.

The proximity of senior staff ensures the right people share information, but the war room concept itself fosters a culture of decision-taking, ensuring that the campaign is always acting. Crucially, it means that campaigns operate at a fast pace, and also that they can rapidly adapt to changing circumstances.[81] For these reasons, the war room is also the place where the campaign *learns*. In such a climate, where people share and discuss information, in taking decisions and discussing the effects of those decisions the campaign staff go through a period of accelerated learning about what works and does not – and this in turn produces better decisions next time.

POPULARISATION OF THE CONCEPT

The concept was made popular in politics by President Bill Clinton's 1992 campaign, managed by James Carville. They created the war room to deal with hesitancy and indecision as a result of excessive bureaucracy in the early days of the campaign. Too many advisers were saying too many things to the candidate and decisions were not being made. The creation of the war room at the Little Rock campaign HQ in Clinton's home state of Arkansas changed things dramatically.

The war room was a perfect way to bring order to the chaos of campaign life – to the massive flow of information coming in, the inevitable bureaucratic challenges, and the endless demands from a 24-hour media. By 1992, the complexity of campaign life was such that a new decision-taking process was required and the war room was the answer.

James Carville explained the rationale for the war room in the following way:

> "The war room was designed for action... In the past, campaigns were rigid hierarchies. They were eleven-story buildings, with the grassroots folks on the bottom floor and layers and layers of intermediary authority until, finally, you got to the top, where the decisions were made. So if an idea wanted to make its way from the bottom to the top, by the time it got to the guy with the secret key to the executive washroom, there were ten floors of

functionaries who saw it as their duty to kill it... So we changed the structure to shift the onus. Every department within the campaign had a representative in the war room: the research and political and press and policy and media and polling and speechwriting teams were at the heart of it, but the administrative and fundraising and legal folks were there, too."[82]

Due to the 1992 campaign working so well, and because most campaigns these days talk about their own war rooms, it can look like a deceptively easy concept to master. It is simple, as all the best ideas are, but not easy to get right. Too many people in campaigns and the corporate world assume that the war room works simply as an open-plan office. This is wrong, and it is why I stress above the point that it is partly about physical space but partly too about mentality.

You can have an open-plan office, even one that collects the key senior staff in one place, but if decisions cannot be taken because real power lies elsewhere, for example with the candidate on the road, you do not have a war room but instead an open-plan office. Conversely, you can have an office building housing all the senior staff in a series of small offices, but you have a war room concept if senior staff are near to each other, constantly talking and constantly taking decisions.

Another misconception about the role of the war room is that it is primarily for rebuttal. Much of the analysis of the Clinton 1992 effort, and of the Labour imitation of it in the UK in the 1997 election, focused on this aspect of the war room's function. This is because this is the part the media is most aware of – they are, or were at least, the primary recipients of the rebuttal materials sent out by the early war rooms.

Effective rebuttal is extremely important in a campaign – if anything, it is more important with the rapid growth of the web and social media – but effective rebuttal is the by-product of a more fundamental and important benefit. This is that the war room allows campaigns to take a whole manner of decisions more quickly.

Rebuttals come quickly because the right people are in the room to see what is important in the ongoing debate, to commission research or the simple retrieval of information, and to take a decision to push contradictory information out into the real world. Similarly, a war room capability should also allow better and quicker decisions to be taken on everything from future advertising spends, to where the candidate should be spending his or her time, to potential changes to the campaign's message.

James Carville explained the importance of being able to retrieve information and act on it in an account of the 1992 campaign, written shortly after it had finished:

> "Information is the major weapon in a political campaign, and the new headquarters in Little Rock had to be a place where someone knew everything there was to know. We had the technology, we had the information, and we could bring it out and use it whenever and wherever we wanted. So much of what happens in a campaign is that you have information, but unless it's instantly retrievable it doesn't do you any good. You're always fighting deadlines. Time is your enemy, and I had to come up with a way that we could really get people wired up."[83]

THE MILITARY RATIONALE FOR THE WAR ROOM

The campaign war room concept is crucial for businesses. The chaotic and unpredictable effects of the rise of opinion demand businesses develop a decision-taking capability with an emphasis on speed and adaptability. In a later section we will look at how firms can recreate this concept in their own communications operations.

However, as businesses consider how to emulate campaigns' success in decision-taking, they will struggle to find additional explanatory theory on why the war room concept works so well. Quite simply, campaign consultants have never taken the time to explain it to the outside world. For this reason, businesses need to look to the sector that inspires many in politics in the first place – the military. The war room is, after all, essentially a command centre in the model of a military operation.

Anyone that doubts this should visit the Churchill War Rooms in London, next to HM Treasury by St James's Park.[84] Developed as an underground command centre for Winston Churchill in the Second World War, the Cabinet War Rooms (as they were known) brought together key decision-takers and advisers who could help Churchill to continue to take decisions when it was too dangerous to operate above ground in Whitehall.

It is one of the world's great museums and an interesting intellectual experience, showing an efficient decision-taking facility designed to keep the British war effort moving. It illustrates the point that you do not necessarily need to have an entire bureaucracy together at any one time to take decisions – a war room that contains the most senior staff with the *ability and authority to take decisions* is enough.

Two theoretical concepts help us understand the rationale for the war room and its ability to help organisations transform their decision-taking. US strategist John Boyd's intellectual work on his *OODA loop* – well known to many in Western military circles – explains the importance of the rapid processing of important information in chaotic operating climates. The focus of the US Marine Corps (USMC) on *decentralised decision-taking* explains the importance of delegation and trust of junior staff in the rapid execution of decisions.

BOYD'S OODA LOOP

Relatively unknown outside the military, strategist John Boyd is considered to be one of the best pilots ever produced by the USAF (US Air Force). As Boyd's career developed and he became more focused on the theory behind conflict, he became increasingly influential on the thinking of the USMC, well known for its interest in new ideas and innovation. Boyd left little formal written work behind, though his ideas are to be found in a series of presentations he made in the last few decades of the last century and in the work of those who admired his thinking.[85]

The key concept Boyd is best remembered for is the OODA loop. The concept explains how organisations take the right decisions fast in times of chaos. The concept suggests organisations *observe* their operating environment, pulling in as much information as possible. They then *orient* to their environment, essentially processing information and deciding what is important and relevant and what is not. The organisation then *decides* what it is going to do and then *acts* in order to do it. Observe – Orient – Decide – Act.

Essentially, this is the same process that occurs in the campaign war room. Campaigns *observe* through extensive monitoring systems designed to ensure senior staff know exactly what is going on at all times. Staff make sure they read every relevant magazine and newspaper and watch every news channel. These days they also ensure they follow relevant blogs and social media platforms. In addition, trackers following opposition candidates will feed back information from the campaign trail.

Campaigns then *orient* to this inflow of information. They consider whether the information coming in materially changes the operating climate and the balance of power in public debate. They work out whether their general assumptions about the campaign have changed, whether their strategy remains appropriate, and whether specific plans need to be changed. If so, the campaign's senior staff will take a *decision* and *act*. They will then *observe* the reaction through their general monitoring, and *orient* to this inflow of information. And so the OODA loop is repeated.

The lessons for campaigns here are obvious. Without doing so consciously, through their war rooms political campaigns create an environment to execute Boyd's OODA loop effectively. The war room helps the campaign to pull in information, process it and decide what is important, take decisions and learn from it all, and then begin the process again.

The disjointed campaign model seen in the past – particularly in the UK – with people on different sites and an opaque decision-taking process (to be fair, still a big problem in the UK), made the efficient execution of the OODA loop impossible. Students of campaigns and corporate communications should consider Boyd's work carefully.

DECENTRALISED DECISION-TAKING

It may seem at first that the war room is about *centralising* all decision-taking. This is not the intention. Rather, the war room is about taking the right high-level decisions on the basis of the right information – decisions that give the rest of the operation overall direction such that they can take their own decisions in their own areas to ensure progress is being made. The war room ultimately encourages and facilitates *decentralised decision-taking*.

Decentralised decision-taking is taken extremely seriously in the military and it has become an integral part of the US military's thinking, particularly in the USMC, where they have practised a rapid, fast-paced form of combat known as *maneuver warfare*. This is the use of fast, constant forward movement to drive deep into enemy territory before they can respond.

The USMC have become expert in this on a massive scale. They were at the tip of the spear in the ground invasion of Iraq in 2003, driving deep into the country in the space of a very short period of time. As with Boyd's OODA loop, it is worth spending time studying the USMC's application of maneuver warfare in relation to its creation of the right machine.

Jason Santamaria, Vincent Martino and Erik Clemons wrote an unusual and useful guide to the application of maneuver warfare to the corporate world: *The Marine Corps Way: Using Maneuver Warfare to Lead a Winning Organization*.[86] In it, they highlight guiding principles for the translation of the USMC philosophy into business management. The key guiding principle for us here, and one which will help campaigns and businesses make the war room concept work, is decentralised decision-taking.

Decentralised decision-taking is a way of increasing the speed of decision-taking, allowing an organisation to move forward faster. Achieving it is more difficult than it sounds. This is what the authors of *The Marine Corps Way* have to say about it:

> "The aim is to give those closest to the action the latitude to take advantage of on-the-spot information unavailable to their superiors. While midlevel and frontline leaders are strongly encouraged to make decisions on their own and act on them, their actions must be consistent with the organization's overall objectives. To this end decentralized decision making relies heavily on the commander's intent – the leader's desired final result – to define the scope of initiative that subordinates can exercise."

They go on:

> "A risk-reward trade-off in its own right, decentralized decision making can deliver breakthrough results by increasing the likelihood of non-linear accomplishments – situations in which an extraordinary act by an individual disproportionately determines the course of large-scale competitive encounters. But it also carries considerable risk: distributed authority is, by nature, chaotic and can result in a higher prevalence of mistakes, especially when overzealous junior leaders do not act in concert with the commander's intent. To reap the full rewards of decentralized decision making, the leader must be willing to trust the capabilities of his or her subordinates, relinquish some degree of control, and resist the temptation to intervene when execution is not as precise as he or she would like."[87]

In practice, the authors suggest that the way to make decentralised decision-taking work is by communicating the commander's intent, issuing "mission orders" and ensuring leaders explain why a specific course of action has been developed. That means arming subordinates with a sense of the overall strategy, so that ultimately all staff, in any given event within that campaign, will know how their reaction will affect the overall mission.

With this shared sense of strategy, a junior staff member that witnesses a particular event that has a bearing on the organisation's ability to achieve its goal would know what action is required to affect that unfolding event. Mission orders are the inevitable result of this culture, where subordinates are told what their objective is, but given considerable freedom to meet that objective in their own way.

DECISION-*TAKING*, NOT DECISION-*MAKING*

In this chapter I have consistently used the term decision-*taking* rather than decision-*making*. Here, I follow the lead of Dr Jamie MacIntosh, director of programmes at the Institute for Security & Resilience Studies of University College London.[88] Dr MacIntosh, a former British Army officer who became a senior adviser to Lord John Reid before becoming an academic, believes the distinction is important for people who are serious about creating effective machines.

MacIntosh argues decision-making implies the process where large numbers of people in a bureaucracy come together to *make* decisions in the abstract, while not actually having to take decisions themselves and be responsible for them. In other words, they are the actual decisions that advisers come to. Decision-taking, on the other hand, is about action – taking a decision that has a real-world impact and consequences for the person taking it. MacIntosh says:

> "Differentiating decision-making from decision-taking might seem like semantic hair splitting but having been a participant observer in several strategic decisions there are important issues at stake. Decisive moments arrive when uncertainty is irreducible. This is the point at which decisions need to be taken. Such moments may be

anticipated or not; they may be slow or fast onset. Support to decision-takers may involve some rational risk calculus or more intricate judgements. This is the work of decision-makers; they can inform but not take decisions. Collective decisions tend to blur the distinction between decision-takers and decision-makers. A consensus is easy to arrive at where uncertainty can be dispelled, although this happy circumstance is not a decisive moment.

"Conversely, when uncertainty is irreducible too many find it convenient to hide in a confusion of overlapping authorities and responsibilities. This becomes all too clear in the aftermath of botched decisions. A decision-taker earns their leadership role because they take responsibility for their actions in the face of irreducible uncertainty. Decision-makers need not be that courageous."[89]

Those people that have held ultimate responsibility for a decision, even a small one, know the distinction is important. Whenever I work with younger staff members on the rise who assume positions of responsibility, I always tell them that one of the biggest decisions they will take in their careers is when they sign off the copy and details on their business card without having a boss look over it first. In the past, decisions made were checked by more senior people – when you are the ultimate decision-taker, even signing off a business card, you enter a new world.

IMPLEMENTING THESE LESSONS

The lessons we have seen here from the world of political communications and from the military are undoubtedly directly relevant to those people working in corporate communications and public affairs, and particularly so given the explosion of opinion.

The growth of the web has created a more chaotic, unpredictable environment for communications and public affairs teams and many businesses operate in a state of near-permanent crisis, constantly shaping their external reputation and outsiders' perceptions of their key issues.

Like campaigns and the military, businesses must therefore structure their teams and position themselves correctly in the wider organisation in such a way that they can take the right decisions quickly. They must be fast and adaptable and they must learn as they go along from what works and what does not.

What does this mean in practice?

Above all it means businesses must consider the recreation of the war room concept in their own organisations. It also means that they must spend significant time and resources investing in their own staff and creating a culture of decentralised decision-taking. Rapid and adaptable decision-taking depends on the senior staff trusting more junior staff to respond to unfolding scenarios as they see fit. Junior staff can only do this if they have a clear sense of strategy, an intuitive understanding of the general approach that the senior staff take and of the businesses' wider culture, and also tactical competence.

CREATING A WAR ROOM

Before establishing the war room, it is vital organisations meet a prerequisite: the war room must have the authority to take decisions so it can respond at no notice to shape opinion. Without this authority, there is no point spending time and resources creating the war room.

Some firms have this already, with the chief executive allowing the director of communications and/or director of public affairs to speak on behalf of the business without constantly seeking approval, even on controversial matters. However, there are still too many businesses with excessively bureaucratic processes where a huge amount of time is taken to clear simple quotes, let alone anything on a controversial issue.

We see this regularly in the corporate world when businesses come under external attack from hostile groups or individuals, with allegations of poor ethics. Under such circumstances, even where the allegations are unfair, many businesses find it hard to push back because their corporate culture insists that everything that goes out publicly is signed off by a combination of the most senior executives and lawyers.

Dealing with public opinion and developing the war room concept requires that the senior management of the organisation trust the directors of communications and public affairs to operate freely without having to check everything, just as they would the chief operations officer, or other senior staff. While businesses can agree a bank of comments and quotes in advance, this is a second-rate solution. Directors of communications and public affairs can only protect the business' reputation in this new world if they have the authority to act as they see fit. By the time they are given permission, it will be too late.

Once this prerequisite has been met, the war room can be constructed. I prefer what you might call a pure war room, with relevant staff sitting together in a single open-plan office, as I find everyone being able to hear each other's thoughts and conversations to be extremely useful in creating a shared outlook. In my view this is the best way for people to develop a sense for what is going on and ensure decisions are taken quickly. Most businesses will be small enough to make this possible – few organisations outside of the mega campaigns will have so many communications and public affairs staff that they need to be on different floors.

It will be down to the senior staff in the operation to decide who fits into the war room. There can be relatively few fixed positions, and these may change over time depending on the nature of the challenges a business faces. For example, the make up of the war room might be different when a business is dealing with, say, a major product recall (when technical staff might play a prominent role) to when it is dealing with a worker strike (when internal communications staff or HR staff might be more important).

Senior staff also need to consider how the war room works with the rest of the business. In a political campaign, the war room is the most important part of the organisation because they *are* a communications operation. Businesses, however, are focused on selling their goods and services and making profit. The senior war room staff must therefore find a way of reporting into the board structure without undermining their day-to-day operational independence on most issues (the biggest issues will inevitably be referred upwards).

The senior staff in the war room will also have to ensure that they are sufficiently plugged into other crucial members of staff for whom it does not make sense to be in the war room. For example, while it makes sense for someone from the legal team to sit in a campaign war room, it does not necessarily make sense in the corporate world. The same might be true for staff from the product development teams, the finance team, the HR team and so on.

The war room must, however, be able to take the right decisions. Keeping Boyd's thinking in mind, it must be able to observe, orient, decide and act. Through intelligent chains of meetings and close relationships, senior war room staff must make sure the right intelligence is coming in and that they have a sense for how their own decisions are going to affect others in the business.

A CULTURE FOR DECENTRALISED DECISION-TAKING

Creating effective decentralised decision-taking is partly about organisational design but it is also a cultural issue. It depends on the creation of a permanent *learning culture* – where people are expected and encouraged to take decisions and calculated risks while also formally learning new skills. Staff must never worry that reasonable missteps resulting from taking responsibility will lead to sanctions in the form of reduced career prospects or even dismissal. In other words, there needs to be a culture of learning and trust.

In this way, doing and learning is the most important aspect of building this culture. If they are in the war room, staff will benefit from the organisational learning that takes place as the business takes decisions and observes the response. Regardless of their closeness to the centre of decision-taking, staff need to be given regular feedback on their performance and on the impact of the decisions they are taking. Senior management must therefore ensure that staff are not just *doing*, but that they are *learning* too.

However, businesses need to take a more formal approach to their staff training too and start teaching new skills to help staff development. People who work in corporate communications and public affairs are mostly expected to learn the skills of their trade on the job. People who take more senior positions are, for the most part, expected to be something approaching the finished article. We are anything but.

Businesses must therefore ensure all staff fully understand the organisation's philosophy, general strategy and specific plans. They must ensure staff know the organisation's objectives at a given moment, as well as their own. Staff must know how their role fits into the wider organisation and what is expected of them.

But the communications industry must also start taking the teaching of communications skills more seriously. Communications teams must supplement their standard induction programmes and their own processes for sharing information on strategy and planning with their own programmes to teach communications skills – for instance an Advanced Course in Communications.

The skills that I have set out in this book are those that I believe are most important in affecting public opinion. But other businesses, particularly those in other sectors, will have their own concerns. For example, some might wish to emphasise how to display information visually, or how to create great presentations. The course would include detailed analyses of case studies of where things have worked well or failed and would also include regular war gaming to help communications staff to encourage students to think hard for themselves. While the course would be graded, the overwhelming objective would be to get students to think critically to help them become more creative and more adaptable. (A sketch course is set out in the Appendix.)

This course would be a communications equivalent to the Adaptive Leaders' Course sketched out by former USMC officer Don Vandergriff in his interesting short book from 2005, *Raising the Bar*. Vandergriff's course was designed to help officers think better and act better. He rightly points out that such a course has relevance for people who work in politics.[90]

Thinking about a climate that encourages rapid decision-taking, it goes without saying this depends on a culture that encourages people to take the initiative and to take risks, but also to ask for guidance where appropriate. A culture of negativity where people worry about taking decisions because they might feel stupid will kill creativity and effective decision-taking, so too will a culture which is seen to punish mistakes and reward caution. It is better for a firm to keep power completely concentrated at the top than to try to decentralise in a culture of fear.

Businesses must also reward – and be seen to reward – staff who show creativity and take risks. The best staff should be given additional responsibilities and financial rewards for success. Creativity and risk taking should formally be rewarded in staff appraisals and risk aversion should be noted and commented on. When things go wrong after creative staff have taken a calculated risk, they should not be criticised but told to keep trying to push things forward.

CHANGING YOUR TEAM

The war room raises big questions about the way businesses structure their communications teams to deal with the rise of opinion. Usually, larger companies have separate teams and separate budget lines for their marketing and advertising teams to their corporate communications and public affairs teams. The new media teams tend to sit in the marketing and advertising teams but often the corporate communications and public affairs teams will have access to the Facebook and Twitter accounts.

The rationale for this divide is the marketing and advertising teams create the overall brand and image of the business, operating on a longer-term basis, while the corporate communications and public affairs teams are responsible for short to medium-term reputation issues. The advertising and marketing teams also speak directly to customers and make them aware of new products, offers and so on.

The rise of opinion completely changes communications – in its broadest sense – for businesses. As we have seen, for many, the daily challenges to their reputation on the web and social media are so serious they can undermine the careful branding exercises that businesses go through on a regular basis. For many businesses, the daily shaping of their reputation is the most important thing for their reputation. Businesses should therefore start to create far more integrated communications teams than they might otherwise, linking a core of them together through the war room concept.

It makes sense for many to fit their communications staff under experienced directors of communications who are responsible for the overall reputation of the business – like the campaign manager in a political campaign. That is not to suggest advertising and marketing teams should all of a sudden focus on the day-to-day reputation management of a firm – clearly longer-term brand and image creation are crucial – but increasingly it lacks credibility to think of communications like many businesses do. (In the conclusion, I set out the case for a much more integrated approach that reflects the campaign model.)

Furthermore, the challenges thrown up by the rise of opinion mean businesses need to think differently about the sort of people that make the best communications staff. Currently, the sorts of people that businesses recruit into these roles are highly creative, good at writing, verbally gifted and collaborative. This makes sense when you are dealing with the established media and they are very positive skills to have in any part of a business in any case.

But given that the rise of opinion is making communications a more confrontational and aggressive job, in which large numbers of people are holding businesses to account on virtually every part of their operations, businesses need to start recruiting people into communications jobs who, frankly, know how to fight. They need to go after the same people who are working in campaigns.

There are two types of people found to an unusually large degree in campaigns that businesses should look at hiring – those skilled at grassroots politics, particularly online, and policy researchers. They will help businesses get an edge in the aggressive world they are going to find themselves in over time.

Grassroots specialists will be useful to businesses as they start forming alliances and campaigns online and elsewhere with people interested in those issues in which the business takes an interest. As we will see later, these sorts of alliances are crucial to businesses in protecting their reputation. These people also have a good understanding for how to engage directly with the public, leading conversation and pushing back where necessary without going over the edge into aggression.

Policy researchers will be useful in providing information for instant and intelligent response to those who are either criticising the business directly, or who are shaping debate on issues that the operation cares about in such a way that the business looks bad. While emotion in argument counts, people watching conversations taking place online want to know that one group or another has the facts on its side. In online debate, it is extraordinary how quickly *facts* – real or imagined – take hold.

Whoever businesses ultimately decide to take on in their reformed teams, they must remember that having smooth PR professionals to persuade journalists and stakeholders to say nice things is becoming less important than persuading lower-middle-class people sitting at their computers in suburbia of the merits of their case. A genuine mix of skills is required.

CHAPTER SEVEN
CREATING EFFECTIVE STRATEGY

WHAT IS STRATEGY AND WHY DOES IT MATTER?

THROUGHOUT THIS BOOK, I have tried to make clear that the explosion of opinion online creates a completely new operating climate for businesses. Firms now come face to face with ordinary people in public conversation and they must communicate in a world that is faster-moving, aggressive, emotional and above all *uncertain*.

In the last chapter, we saw how competent decision-taking and organisational design can help businesses to cut through this uncertainty and maintain momentum so they are constantly influencing public attitudes. This is one of the two fundamental *operational* skills that businesses must learn from political campaigns. The other is the creation of effective strategy.

Unfortunately, if you use the word *strategy* in a meeting in much of the corporate communications world people will roll their eyes in exasperation. Strategy has become identified with excessive and unnecessary complexity, endless irrelevant talking and planning, and inaction. Those organisations that talk the most about strategy are usually the most dysfunctional.

Why? Ultimately, it comes down to a widespread lack of understanding about what strategy is and an inability to construct it. In his book *Good Strategy Bad Strategy*, corporate consultant Richard Rumelt airs his frustration that strategy has lost its meaning in the modern world as people use it to mean pretty much anything they want it to mean. He argues the concept, "has been stretched to a gauzy thinness as pundits attach it to everything from utopian visions to rules for matching your tie with your shirt."[91]

In communications and right across the corporate world, vast numbers of people now have the word *strategy* in their job title or in their job description for no apparent reason, and increasing numbers of actions are now described as being strategic. If it is more than a couple of weeks away, or requires thinking and planning, any action will have strategy applied. Rumelt explains:

> "Despite the roar of voices wanting to equate strategy with ambition, leadership, 'vision', planning, or the economic logic of competition, strategy is none of these. The core of strategy work is always the same: discovering the critical factors in a situation and designing a way of coordinating and focusing actions to deal with those factors."[92]

He adds:

> "A good strategy has an essential logical structure that I call the kernel. The kernel of a strategy contains three elements: a diagnosis, a guiding policy, and coherent action. The guiding policy specifies the approach to dealing with the obstacles called out in the diagnosis. It is like a sign-post, marking the direction forward but not defining the details of the trip. Coherent actions are feasible coordinated policies, resource commitments, and actions designed to carry out the guiding policy."[93]

Strategy is the realistic, flexible, high-level approach taken to achieve a stated goal – an approach that considers obstacles and challenges that can be identified in advance and anticipated, and that enables and encourages the organisation to adapt to changing circumstances. Rather than standing in the way of action, therefore, the creation of strategy *facilitates* it.

The practical differences between those organisations with a clear strategy and those without are stark, and particularly so where they face serious external challenges. Organisations with a clear strategy know what they want to achieve and how. They are able to give staff guidance on the approach they are expected to take, to plan their activity, allocate resources accordingly and respond to rapidly changing circumstances. They are able to create and maintain momentum and they stand a chance of dictating the public agenda.

Those organisations without a clear strategy regularly find themselves on the back foot. Without a clear sense for what it is they are trying to achieve, they end up responding day-to-day and hour-to-hour to the actions of others. While they may display flashes of competence in a given scenario, they will not reap the benefits of their actions because success will not necessarily push the organisation towards achieving their preferred objectives.

Dr Jamie MacIntosh argues strategy makes a real impact on the success of any organisation because it helps it to chart a course amid an uncertain operating climate. It helps an organisation to keep taking decisions and move forward, and helps it exploit opportunities as they arise. He says:

> "Distinguishing good from bad strategy seems easier in retrospect. Of course, what makes strategy vital is the approach to the future. This is also what makes strategy difficult and prone to being done badly. When uncertainties abound, the illusion of certainty or resignation to chance are attractive postures. Sometimes these postures are lucky. Fixating on certainty in either the environment or the performance of habits offers some advantages. Likewise, celebrating the talented few who can adapt fast to unknowable contingencies can pay-off.

> "Both postures miss too much of what is important to business. Over reliance on continuity or the talents of a

narrow few ingrains competitive disadvantages. Strategies that work confound expectations because they harness both continuity and change in winning combinations. This requires agility, versatility and stamina whether differentiating the fitness of what your business offers or even shaping the environment so that your fitness grows and excels more radically. Catching up with change is what habit obliges followers to do. Strategy done well advances changes in more fitting businesses that lead the way into the future."[94]

THE EFFECTIVE USE OF STRATEGY IN CAMPAIGNS

Good political campaigns are obsessed with creating a credible strategy. Operating in a chaotic and uncertain public conversation, where they must simultaneously try to influence opinion while dealing with endless attacks and competing narratives, means they need to know exactly what it is they want to achieve. They know without a clear strategy to guide their action they will end up reacting to every story that comes up in completely inconsistent ways. The public will end up having no idea of their priorities or what they stand for.

In practical terms, the creation of strategy helps campaigns take the right decisions over time to define themselves publicly, and to define those issues most important to them. It means that opposition groups and sceptics are forced to respond from a relatively weaker position and those with an open mind are more likely to be influenced in a positive direction. Momentum is an extremely important force in communications.

Good campaigns have Rumelt's *kernel*. They have a diagnosis – a reading of the opinion polls and an understanding of their relative strengths and weaknesses in relation to the opposition. They have a guiding policy – messages that they want to develop to persuade the public and a set of audiences which are most important. Finally, they have a clear plan of action – a coherent grid/forward planner.

NORTH EAST SAYS NO

One of the best campaigns I have worked on was the North East Says No (NESNO) campaign, which derailed the Labour government's plans for Regional Assemblies across England by winning a public referendum in the North East on the issue in November 2004. Despite being massively outspent by a Yes campaign backed by the entire left-leaning political establishment of the region, NESNO won an unexpected landslide – by nearly 80% to 20% – with the polls at the start of the campaign pointing to a big Yes vote. This was achieved in large measure by a clear and effective strategy that guided campaign action.

After extensive desk research and polling, our diagnosis was clear. We faced three main challenges. Firstly, the North East as a region leaned overwhelmingly left and, with minor exceptions, had widespread hostility to the Conservative Party. Secondly, the polls showed broad support for more local powers for the North East. Thirdly, we knew the Yes campaign would have more resources generally and more money specifically.

There were some big positives too. We had the support of large numbers of businesspeople in the North East. Also, the polls showed public support fell away when people heard the Regional Assembly would be expensive but have little real power – and midway through Labour's second term, the growing discontent with the political class nationally was mirrored by discontent locally with the Labour Party.

Finally, because everyone thought we were going to lose, all the egomaniacs and self-proclaimed experts stayed out of what they assumed was going to be a fiasco. This allowed us to put in place an extremely focused, lean and fast-moving campaign with no outside interference. Decision-taking was rapid in our organisation.

Our guiding action was therefore the following: to create an aggressive earned media campaign that was not only outside party politics but hostile towards it, using independent businesspeople to make the case that the Regional Assembly would simply raise taxes to pay for more politicians with no power. Our campaign slogan summed this up nicely: "Politicians Talk, We Pay". Having confidence in the power of our messages, we assumed that all but the most committed yes voters were up for grabs, and that we had to generate as much coverage as possible, wherever we could.

The campaign launched formally in early September 2004, with postal votes due to be sent out to voters in the middle of October, and the ballot closing at the start of November. Our plan split the campaign into two. Firstly, we would target more interested voters – people we judged would vote early – on issues showing the Assembly would cost a fortune and that it had no power. Secondly, we would target those voters more likely to be driven by anti-politician sentiment by stressing that it would only lead to more, full-time, professional politicians.

Our main spokespeople – John Elliot, Ian Dormer and Graham Robb – delivered clear messages in excellent TV interviews day after day. They were helped by a number of creative stunts the campaign designed. For example, we burned millions of pounds of fake £50 notes – adding up to the annual cost of the Assembly – in front of TV cameras. We launched a 15ft-high inflatable white elephant – the *white elephant* Assembly – and placed campaign staff in overalls and hard hats next to hired diggers to start work on the new *palace for politicians*. Our referendum broadcast was a cheap, raw and extremely effective film featuring local people airing brutally frank views on the political class.[95]

Guided by a strategy that the team was confident in, the campaign secured immediate traction. The combination of well-executed made-for-TV stunts, with competent interviews and a steady stream of campaign-generated print stories meant we pulled ahead in the polls just ahead of postal votes arriving at people's homes. An extremely aggressive push back by the Yes campaign – primarily focused on linking us to the Tories – only played into our hands by turning this into an unpleasant spectacle that the public associated with politics at its worse. When the results were announced, it was a wipeout.

Clearly, our victory depended on the effective implementation of a plan. Had our spokespeople been beaten regularly in interviews or had our stunts gone wrong, we would never have secured such decent coverage. However, we would never have been in a position to deliver a good campaign had we not created a thoughtful, clear and effective strategy. At every point in the campaign we knew what we needed to achieve – and this meant decisions could be taken quickly that we knew would have the right impact.

In theory, it should be easier to create effective strategy in smaller-scale campaigns where bureaucracy is less of a problem and people can get on with the campaign. In my experience, that is not the case. The smallest campaigns can be mired in confusion, while the biggest campaigns can function smoothly. At the other end of the spectrum, Barack Obama's last presidential campaign was an extremely well-planned and well-managed campaign, dependent on a clear strategy.

OBAMA 2012 PRESIDENTIAL CAMPAIGN

Just after the election in November 2012, the *Wall Street Journal* had an excellent overview of the Obama campaign's communications strategy:

> "One Sunday in May, Mr. Messina, the manager of President Barack Obama's re-election campaign, went to the president along with other top advisers and proposed an unorthodox strategy. The campaign, he said, wanted to spend heavily, starting immediately, on ads blasting away at Republican nominee Mitt Romney. The idea, explained to the president in a PowerPoint presentation in the Roosevelt Room, was to shape voters' impressions with a heavy expenditure before Mr. Romney had the money to do it for himself.

"The plan defied conventional wisdom, which said a campaign should start slowly with a positive message and save money for the stretch run. And it could leave the president exposed later. 'If it doesn't work, we're not going to have enough money to go have a second theory in the fall,' Mr. Messina said, according to people in the meeting. The president gave his approval. And within weeks the Obama campaign was blasting away in a late-spring offensive, forcing Mr. Romney to respond to charges about his business record and personal finances rather than making the president defend his record."[96]

The Obama campaign's communications strategy was clear. In a year when voters were overwhelmingly focused on the economy, when President Obama himself had no real record to run on (with the US suffering from high unemployment and slow growth), and when Governor Romney was considered by many to have a record turning around corporations, the strategy was to neutralise the issue of the economy and win on other issues and turnout. This is exactly what happened.

The preemptive strike on the economy put Governor Romney on the back foot immediately. President Obama's early strike focused on the less friendly aspects of the hard-nosed private equity industry and helped turn a Romney positive into a negative. When Romney got around to dealing with his private equity baggage and articulating a credible economic plan, he was unable to gain traction for it. President Obama's foreign policy positions and the general social policy positions of the Democrats meant the Obama campaign was better positioned in communications and message terms into November. Their brilliant turnout operation helped them through.

BUSH'S 2004 REELECTION CAMPAIGN

President Obama's 2012 strategy was not so different to the strategy developed in 2004 by George W. Bush's reelection campaign. Under

Karl Rove's overall direction, the campaign also developed a strategy that combined a direct appeal to general voters – this time on national security issues, still huge a short time after 9/11 and amid the wars in Afghanistan and Iraq – and a micro targeting campaign designed to get every possible Republican sympathiser out to vote on election day. This ultimately ensured they carried those traditionally Republican areas that had begun to inch in the Democrats' favour, like Virginia, but also to win genuine toss-up states like ever-troublesome Florida.

Writing in his memoir, *Courage and Consequence*, Karl Rove explained the strategy of the 2004 Bush reelection campaign:

> "Our biggest challenge was to find voters who would swing to our side in a country that had grown more partisan and divided since we had arrived in Washington. The problem was not just Democratic activists who had never recovered from the 2000 outcome and who had developed a pathological hatred of Bush. The country itself had retreated into two very firm camps... The election would not just be about mobilizing Republican and Republican-leaning independents, but about converting the few swing voters who were out there. The most important of the swing voters were suburban women, particularly those who were married and between the ages of thirty-five to fifty with kids."[97]

He added later, "Our convention goals were simple: portray Bush as a strong wartime leader, and focus on the future."[98]

OVERCOMING SCEPTICISM IN THE CORPORATE WORLD

Now they are exposed to public opinion in the same way as political campaigns, and with the operating climate being so much more uncertain, businesses are going to have to become as focused on the creation of communications strategies as political campaigns.

Businesses need the same levels of momentum in public debate to affect opinion.

The corporate world, like the military, is known for its obsession with strategy. Go into any major bookshop and there are likely to be shelves of books on corporate strategy. Some will be purely academic, some will seek to update past classics like *The Prince* or *The Art of War,* some will apply military lessons to the corporate world, some will be more biographical. While Richard Rumelt laments widespread lack of strategic understanding amongst many businesses, there is certainly attention paid to the area.

However, this deep interest in strategy at the operational level in corporate life has not been translated into corporate communications and public affairs. In the world of communications, political campaigns have shown a much greater interest in – and grasp of – strategy than those that work in corporate communications.

In my experience, few businesses create communications strategy in the same clear way that campaigns do, usually for three reasons. Firstly, many businesses find it difficult to list their communications priorities, even to themselves. They worry that saying one thing is a priority means that something else is not a priority and therefore risks upsetting all of those people who work in that area. Businesses often just create lists of priorities designed to please everybody in the organisation – a list that includes so many things there are in fact no priorities and the *strategy* created is meaningless. This is particularly common in very large organisations.

Secondly, many people are reluctant to box themselves into a stated strategy now when there might be a better one that emerges further down the line. They worry when the operating climate is not clear, it is difficult to decide in advance what to do. Such businesses prefer to act on a tactical basis for the foreseeable future until the picture is clearer (which it never is). This is common amongst people who simply do not think strategically. Lots of people find it difficult to think more than a short time ahead and they find it difficult, ultimately, to imagine what success looks like and how to get there.

Thirdly, it is common for people to find creating strategy unsettling in that it implies serious and decisive action on their part, done in full sight. If everyone knows there is a strategy – or at least the senior staff – and everyone is watching how it unfolds, people are inevitably going to be held accountable for the success and failure of it. When there is no visible strategy, mistakes are less visible. Again, in my experience, this is particularly common in larger companies where senior staff worry they might be accountable for a particular strategy which they ultimately do not have sufficient responsibility and power to deliver effectively. In other words, they have all the risk but not necessarily enough tools to deliver – the worst position anyone can be in.

The difference between having a strategy and not having a strategy are enormous. Organisations with strategy lead their staff better, plan better, and take decisions faster and better. People in campaigns often say that it is better to have a bad strategy than no strategy at all, because at least the organisation takes decisions and moves forward. They are not joking. It is genuinely better to have a strategy that you think is solid but not perfect and which allows the machine to function than it is to work without a strategy.

Strategy is really what makes effective decision-taking possible. The war room can only work if people ultimately know what it is they are trying to achieve and what their general approach is. It is no luxury – it is a prerequisite for action.

HOW TO CREATE STRATEGY

The media likes the idea of the strategist going to the mountains for the weekend and coming back with a master plan that perfectly understands how the public and the opposition will react to the campaign's every move. The reality is always messier.

The best campaigns create strategy collaboratively – not in the form of an endless committee process, but by harnessing the ideas and skills of a small group of talented people (that get on with each other). Also, strategy is always an ongoing process – campaigns rarely get it right first time and they will often redo their guiding strategy during the campaign. Businesses should therefore see the creation of strategy as a *process*.

In my experience, the key to a sensible strategy is to focus on the context to establish what Rumelt calls the *diagnosis*. To some extent, the creation of the guiding policy and the setting out of coherent action is *relatively* easy when this has been achieved. It is vital organisations fully consider the operating climate and the people that will affect it. Getting the diagnosis wrong because you are keen to get straight into the specifics of planning will set the whole campaign out on the wrong footing.

As I have just discussed, it is also extremely important organisations self-consciously inject a serious dose of realism into this process. In communications, the best way of doing this is ensuring the strategy-making process is integrated into the message development and campaign planning processes. If the strategy is unrealistic, trying to imagine how messages will play out in the real world or considering ideas for concrete action will soon reveal it.

The process that I would recommend is the following:

1. Commission desk research and opinion research to develop a sense for the operating climate.

2. Run an initial strategy workshop to synthesise the research and develop a working strategy.

3. Run a war game to consider how the strategy will play out.

4. Work on messaging using more opinion research and general stress testing.

5. Create a written strategy which can be agreed and shared amongst the organisation's staff.

I now look at these in more detail.

1. INITIAL RESEARCH

Extensive opinion research and desk research will provide initial but detailed context on the organisation's operating climate. Context is absolutely crucial to the creation of strategy and organisations cannot rush it. It can feel to some like unnecessary worry over what others are doing and saying and a distraction from actually formulating strategy. This is wrong. A proper understanding of the operating climate – what people think about your organisation, issues, leadership team and the big events likely to shape this operating climate – is extremely important.

For this reason, staff should spend significant time looking at the following: who the key players are in the area in question, particularly opposition groups; what people are saying about the area, particularly politicians, other decision-takers and key influencers; what major events are likely to shape the corporate climate or public perceptions in coming months; what other organisations in the same field are trying to achieve or what they have tried in the past. There will no doubt be many other relevant issues.

To supplement this research, the organisation should look for existing opinion research on the area – there is always likely to be some out there. The organisation should commission its own landscape opinion research if possible, with both polling and focus groups, to work out what people think about the area in question.

2. STRATEGY WORKSHOP

Once this research has been completed, organisations should bring together relevant staff to discuss and synthesise the research and start developing a working strategy. After an initial presentation on the research, and a discussion on its implications, a useful exercise to begin formulating strategy is to produce what US campaigns call a *message box*. This is essentially a grid that sets out an organisation's relative strengths and weaknesses in relation to their opposition. In his excellent book *The Candidate*, Samuel Popkin explains the concept:

"It is a simple tool to make sure that the many messages from a campaign are coherent, unified, and account for the actions of the opponent. It is used by organizations such as the National Democratic Institute to train candidates in countries like Iraq, Afghanistan, and Nepal, and by activists and consultants in campaigns all over Europe and Latin America. It is a square divided into four quadrants: What the candidate will say about him- or herself. What the candidate will say about his or her opponent(s). What the opponent(s) will say about him- or herself. What the opponent(s) will say about the candidate."[99]

While Popkin suggests the tool dwells on message – which the organisation will be some way off developing – the tool is designed with strategy in mind. The result of the quadrant will be, after all, a visual representation of the strengths and weaknesses of the organisation in relation to a real or imagined opposition. It enables an organisation to start thinking about what sort of an approach might be appropriate in order to maximise its relative strengths and to deal with, and ideally neutralise, its weaknesses. The discussion that follows from this should see the organisation develop a working strategy.

3. WAR GAMING

The next phase is to test out the working strategy in a *war gaming* (or *scenario planning*) exercise. Commonly used in the private sector to prepare teams for crisis management, war gaming is an extremely useful tool for general strategy making. There are different ways of running such events.

In *The Art of the Long View*, Peter Schwartz, a pioneer of scenario planning in the oil industry, suggests businesses create and consider a number of extremely well-researched potential scenarios or plots to see which seems most likely. He explains his approach is designed to set out stark alternatives for executives to discuss.[100] Dr Jamie

MacIntosh of the Institute for Security & Resilience Studies takes a different, more free-wheeling, approach. Some will find the more formal approach set out in *The Art of the Long View* more suitable for their organisation's challenges, while others will lean towards Dr MacIntosh's approach.

Low-tech, short and intellectually very intense, Dr MacIntosh's sessions – which use Event Driven Scenarios – are designed to get people to think deeply about the strengths and weaknesses of organisations, and to make specific recommendations for action that can be synthesised into a workable strategy.

His sessions begin with a general background discussion on what is going on in a given area, before moving on to a discussion about who the key players are in this area. After people are allocated roles to play, typically two game turns are held where participants say how they would respond to a set of events that flashed up on a screen over a timeline.

Usually one game turn focuses on a short period of time – a period of, say, a year – while one game turn focuses on a longer period of time – say, five years. Some of the events will be the organisation's own activities, while others will be external events, expected and unexpected.

According to Dr MacIntosh:

> "War games work because they can enable people to explore potential futures. This is what strategy is really about; leading the way into a future in which change always triumphs. The word 'war' can be a turn off even if games are among the most interactive and rewarding ways to learn. It is important to focus on how war is a process of competitive and co-operative innovation and that strategy is about how enriching and endangering uncertainty can be. These words are no longer the monopoly of the military; they are gifts for us all to use in exploring futures.

"It would be easy to assume that, building up from tactics to operations, strategic war games would be very big detailed and complicated. However, testing a plan, decision-tree, or the selection and performance of tactics may lend themselves to formal models or simulators but do not provide war games for strategists. Scenario planning is no alternative. Whatever the merits of futurology, a scenario tends to be rich in spurious detail disguising a single plotline.

"Event Driven Scenarios (EDS) produce something different. These are Net Assessment Exercises (NAx) carefully designed to test the decision-taking competencies of organisations (particularly interagency or network enterprises), the competitive advantages of their real capability options and capacity for innovation. Strategic players are not confronted with a blizzard of factoids or dramatic garnish. Instead, they are offered patterns of events and asked to narrate what they will do and how they will learn.

"This simple process elicits many narratives from participants in which they share a rapidly growing appreciation of the art of the possible, not just as individuals but from different perspectives among a web of risky relationships. The EDS process does not claim to be predictive but those who have been through NAx are astonished by how patterns of events come up in reality and how much better placed they are to take decisive actions in concert with diverse colleagues. The EDS process is fun, cheap, scalable and most importantly deals with the reality of the uncertainties with which strategic decision-takers must contend."[101]

What people are left with at the end of these games is a very good sense for how an organisation is positioned to drive through its own strategy as well as to respond to likely or possible events that might take place and affect it. The most important part of the session is the final part, where participants are asked to give two recommendations for action for their own organisation – i.e. the organisation that is running the war game.

These recommendations tend to vary widely, with some participants focusing on issues such as their lack of third party support, their lack of resources to deal with a particular likely event, or their lack of sufficient policy knowledge in an important area. As indicated above, the recommendations form the heart of the strategy document that is produced after.

The exercises work far better if the organisation is willing to bring a small number of outsiders into the game. Having outsiders like trusted journalists, executives from companies in a similar field, former government and party advisers, pollsters and think tank analysts, creates a more dynamic and realistic environment. This is true of strategy-making generally – considering outside views and ideas ultimately produces better and more realistic strategy.

4. MESSAGE CREATION

The importance of injecting realism into strategy making means that message creation should at least begin during this process. As indicated above, while the process of messaging is likely to go on for some time, and no doubt continue as circumstances change, the intelligence gathered from early parts of the process will be useful in sense checking whether the strategy being created is going to work in practice.

The steps taken in creating strategy so far will in turn be useful for the organisation as it starts to create its messages. The organisation will, after all, have spent significant amounts of time considering the general operating climate, likely actions of opposition and third-party groups, and possible external shocks. It will be in a good position to understand what messages are likely to be most suitable for the developing campaign and also have a good idea about what messages are likely to work best with different audiences.

At the heart of the process of creating messages is opinion research. Organisations must devote very significant resources to opinion research if they are serious about creating messages that work. I have already covered this in detail earlier.

However, it is worth considering two additional elements in the process of message creation. Firstly, in order to come up with a draft set of messages for testing in polls and focus groups it will be worth running a discrete messaging session. Such a session would consider the desk research and landscape opinion research that had already taken place and would then force participants to seriously boil down their core arguments to a small number of options.

Secondly, and this probably also runs before the actual message testing research takes place, organisations should practise spokespeople using proposed messages in interview scenarios and defending them. This will again provide an additional useful reality check – messages that sound persuasive in a boardroom can quickly lose credibility when they are played out.

5. WRITING THE PLAN AND THE STRATEGY

The final stage of the process is to work on the basics of the communications plan and begin writing and sharing the strategy. As with the process of message creation, it is worth developing the outlines of a plan at this point to test the credibility of the strategy being developed. Organisations need to know that the strategy that has been created – a strategy that will likely have a particular focus of action – can generate enough activity to bring the campaign to life. While the specific details of the plan can be worked out later, the really big things should be discussed at this point.

The actual writing of the strategy and its communication to the wider team will vary depending on the character of the organisation and above all on the extent to which the organisation has people that can write clear strategy and that actually like reading strategy. Personally, I prefer written strategy as I think it forces people to think hard when they write it and it also gives people the chance to consider it in detail. However, others prefer to present strategy and to answer questions. I have seen both approaches work and both fail.

However, it is vital senior staff agree on the strategy at the outset. No communications campaign can work if there is senior disagreement on strategy. Once agreement has been reached, the strategy must be articulated to the rest of the team. Staff must be left in no doubt about what the organisation is trying to achieve in its campaign.

CHAPTER EIGHT
SHAPING REPUTATION ONLINE

FROM THEORY TO IMPLEMENTATION

THE PROLIFERATION OF opinion online demands businesses focus relentlessly on *people* and develop the same fundamental skills political campaigns use to affect opinion. Businesses that understand how people think, how to influence them and how to create organisations to reach them will be in a better position to lead public conversations around their business.

It is only with that understanding that you can create effective tactics. This does not mean the implementation of the tactics is irrelevant, as the ability of a firm to engage on a day-to-day, hour-to-hour basis will determine how successful they are and businesses should develop or purchase necessary expertise or technology to give them the means to engage. However, it remains important for businesses to put the ends before the means. People first, technology second.

In these final chapters I focus on the most important areas in which businesses need to develop operational expertise to manage their reputations. I begin by looking at the web and social media, before looking at the media, and then at how businesses should handle the regular crises they are faced with these days – the sorts of crises we have seen throughout this book.

THE PRINCIPLES OF EFFECTIVE ONLINE ENGAGEMENT

The web and social media platforms are overwhelmingly where businesses must engage to shape their reputation. For a number of years, I have been helping organisations – some very large, some very small – to develop their online presence to shape public conversation. Sometimes this has involved ramping up social media activity to shape existing conversations. Other times it has involved creating bespoke campaigns designed to develop completely new conversations around key issues.

By following the fundamentals laid out in this book to affect public opinion, and the specific principles set out in this chapter on engaging at the tactical level, these organisations were able to substantially shift public debate in their favour. In some cases, the benefits have been enormous, with clients saving or earning millions of pounds in revenue that had been at stake through decisions set to be taken by people worried about their popularity.

Even in areas where opposition activists are active online, businesses should be confident in their ability to improve their reputation and change the way people talk about their most important issues.

The principles for tactical engagement I set out here are a mix of recommendations to help firms plan campaigns and execute them effectively. Those looking for direct instructions on how to overcome the challenges of the explosion of opinion will be disappointed. In reality, no consultant can credibly provide a straight how-to guide in dealing with the public online. The nature of public conversation is extremely unpredictable and fast-moving and every businesses will have their own specific challenges. There can be no substitute for thinking.

Mark Wallace, now working for one of Britain's biggest online news and comment sites Conservative Home, says:

> "There is no perfect rule of how to communicate and who to communicate with online. Social media are still

evolving and growing, so the field is open to be sculpted by creative communicators. Companies need to be open to experimenting and learning as they go along. How human should your voice be? When does a customer complaint cross the line into vexatious trolling? What is a good output from digital comms? All of these questions are seriously challenging for traditional corporate cultures but we must answer them through trial and error.

"Ultimately it is that flexibility which business may find most difficult to adopt. Relaxing, being willing to experiment, learning to laugh publicly at your own mistakes and most of all letting go of the old idea that you can dictate what people say about you are all facts of life in digital communications."[102]

Businesses must be flexible and the options open to organisations for specific action online are limited only by the creative imagination of the communications teams in place. Facebook Townhalls, 'Ask the CEO' Twitter events, web ads, infomercials, blogs, web forums, online games, email campaigns, downloadable leaflets, webinars, Facebook ads, Google AdWords, search engine optimisation, online books and pamphlets, photostreams, podcasts and an array of other ideas are all open to any operation.

Above all, businesses must focus on the key principles behind effective web engagement. At that point, they will be able to create specific campaigns that work best for them.

TAKE THE DECISION TO ENGAGE

The first step for any business is psychological: senior executives must take the decision to commit to direct conversation with the public. This may sound trivial but, for many, this first step is the biggest of all. While almost all businesses are happy to spend significant sums on advertising and marketing campaigns (including online), many worry about what will happen if they talk to the public directly. There is always a bias towards inaction – risks of doing are amplified and risks of not doing are discounted.

It is easy for consultants to dismiss such fears; they do not have to manage the process or answer to a sceptical senior management. But businesses have to accept reality – the scale of conversation on the web is vast and growing, has a serious impact on their reputation, and will continue with or without their involvement. Businesses have no choice *but* to get involved.

David Wilson, one of Britain's best public affairs consultants, and a former special adviser for Labour in Tony Blair's administration, now directs public affairs at the British Beer & Pub Association. He says:

> "The most significant impact of the growth of the web has been the instantaneous nature of public discourse and the proliferation of channels available for public scrutiny and reaction to corporate activity. Not only do corporates and governments have to be tuned in to web traffic and adapt their communications accordingly they have to be tooled up to respond quickly when criticisms or campaigns take off virally."

He adds:

> "When I started in the industry having a targeted stakeholder communications plan and a traditional media plan focused on the broadsheet influencers and opinion leaders would more than suffice. Now the media strategy must embrace digital with the right tone of voice and be prepared to engage with consumers directly through web channels. Growth in the demands for interactivity – with our MPs, our Governments, and our businesses – requires a dynamic approach to transparency and creativity in execution. It is very exciting for the communications and public affairs industry as it requires a wholly different mindset. In the UK we were relatively slow to assess the

impact of the digital revolution as many of us thought it was a bit of fad initially."[103]

Some people that criticise businesses online can never be won over. The chances are, for example, people who join campaigns attacking big oil firms on the environment will never be persuaded about the merits of the oil firms' operations. But, within reason, it is worth engaging with most people online because public conversation is not wholly about direct participants. Vast numbers of people do not engage personally but watch debates taking place and make their own judgements.

Participating online is therefore not all about winning over hostile individuals, but ensuring large numbers of people are persuaded by arguments they see played out. Businesses should engage online with individuals for the same reason they write blogs and commentary on more mainstream sites – because people will see their views. They must always remember their audience is the normal member of the public – not the passionate opponent.

RESEARCH YOUR CONVERSATION PROPERLY

Before taking steps to ramp up the use of social media, to create new web tools and so on, businesses must be completely clear in their own minds who they want to influence and what they want to achieve. They must ensure their activity has a clear rationale and clear targets. They must start with the most basic questions:

- Who is the ultimate, real world audience for the business?
- Who generally influences that audience online and, potentially, who influences those influencers online?
- Who is currently leading the public conversation about the business online and those issues important to it and what are they saying?
- To what extent is this conversation genuinely affecting the reputation of the business in the eyes of its audience?

Let us imagine we are working with a British private healthcare provider that wants to improve its reputation online. This business has told us they are overwhelmingly worried about what people in government think about them because they are important in deciding whether to allow the business to bid for more contracts. They have a sense their mixed online reputation may cause them problems and would like advice on improving it.

We would ask those basic questions listed above to produce a detailed audit of the conversation on healthcare taking place online, paying particular attention to who was commenting on our client. We would look for any intelligence to indicate which publications, websites and commentators were taken most seriously in government.

We would consider online circulation figures for the main healthcare journals, popular health websites and websites of national newspapers that deal regularly with health stories. We would consider the main commentators on health issues on Twitter and other social media platforms and work out who sees their comments by looking at who subscribes to their various feeds. We would look at the broad healthcare debate taking place on social media and online generally.

At the end of this project, our client would be left with a much better understanding of the general conversation taking place on healthcare and where it affected their operations. We might conclude that while senior government workers took the industry journals with the highest circulation figures most seriously, those journals were visibly influenced by stories of poor care in the mass-circulation tabloids, who in turn were taking material from personal stories circulating via Twitter.

We would therefore conclude that our healthcare business should focus heavily on three things:

1. Generating more opinion online highlighting positive examples of care.
2. Sensitively answering wrongful allegations online of poor care.
3. Liaising more closely with the online journalists on the major tabloids.

Our example would radically enhance our client's ability to improve the conversation taking place about them and affect how they were seen amongst key audiences. Without going through such an operation, our client might have focused purely on trying to secure positive coverage in sceptical journals, rather than going to the root of the problem. With everyone so utterly linked on the web, understanding the dynamics of influence and perception really matters. Every business should follow a similar approach.

BE CLEVER, BUT NOT TOO CLEVER

The research operation described above is intended to help businesses develop a sophisticated understanding of their online operating climate to guide action. It is intended primarily to be *useful* for the business. In my experience with web communications, I have found there is a tendency to reach towards things which are technologically advanced or apparently sophisticated, but which ultimately have no real use.

Too many firms and consultants get distracted by things that merely look or sound good – as if they have one eye on securing positive coverage in niche magazines – without thinking through the impact they will have in the real world. For example, some businesses spend significant time and money developing online tools or games that sound interesting in principle but that appeal to too few people to make them worthwhile.

With online communications, I am sympathetic to those that seek to be ahead of the game by creating tools that have limited immediate use but are likely to become popular in coming months and years, or that improve the collective expertise of a business in ways that will be beneficial elsewhere. After all, someone had to be the first blogger, or be an early adopter of Facebook or Twitter. Businesses always have to ask themselves, though, whether time spent on developing something very clever is really worth it.

For some businesses, it makes sense to develop attractive web videos with high production value. Major airlines, for example, might decide they need things to look extremely professional, to constantly give off a sense of luxury or safety. For businesses positioning themselves at the cutting edge of new thinking, it clearly makes sense to create analytical tools for people to use. For many others, it is money down the drain. Businesses need to be realistic about who their audience is, what they would most find useful and take things from there.

CREATE YOUR PERFECT HOME

One of the themes I have returned to repeatedly is that the explosion of opinion online means businesses must aspire to be the most persuasive voices on their own operations and their issues, rather than behaving as if they were the *only* voice. They must go where debate takes place and engage in debate on platforms owned by others. But they must also have a sanctuary where they can present their own case on their own terms. They must develop a *perfect home*.

Various new media consultants shake their heads at this point. Many tend to be sceptical about the power of businesses' corporate web pages to persuade anyone. After all, by their nature such sites are self-interested and biased. With their corporate branding and tendency to engage in one-way communication, some feel these sites are never likely to be taken seriously. It is seen to be far better to engage in two-way dialogue elsewhere – dialogue with greater credibility and authenticity.

I disagree because businesses, like political campaigns, must have at least somewhere they can make arguments without constant outside challenge. Not only is it important for people passing through to hear a firm's best case – a case that will have been extensively tested – but, for businesses to intervene in debate on external platforms like Twitter, they must have pages that they can link to that display a more detailed argument.

BP's website is an example of a very competent corporate website.[104] (Since their Gulf oil spill, they have produced some excellent online communications.) For a start, the website looks good and is well laid out. Unusually, it also manages to provide a focused message – at the time of writing, on the importance of safety – without crowding out links to other important parts of the site.

Elsewhere, the site provides extensive and well-presented material on the company itself, its services, its commitment to sustainability and important statements made by the company. A social media hub provides links to useful videos and comment. At a time when the business has been widely criticised over the Gulf of Mexico spill, it projects openness, good governance and a commitment to safety. This is a demonstration of how businesses can communicate effectively in a difficult market.

Businesses should not feel the need to choose between engaging online in what are effectively public platforms – like Facebook and Twitter – and making their own case on their own site. Businesses can and should do both.

TAKE CONTENT SERIOUSLY

Corporate websites should not be a place where the lack of public challenge means the bar for the quality of content is lowered, but a place where freedom inspires great content. A business should aspire to ensure anyone paying even a brief visit to one of its web pages becomes more sympathetic to its case.[105]

Unfortunately, too many businesses have developed online content that feels like it has been written for their own staff, or for unrealistically enthusiastic fans of the firm. Content is often excessively technocratic or corporate, too inward-facing, or so relentlessly upbeat that it lacks credibility. Such content is never going to be widely read or shared between readers, and it is unlikely to be persuasive.

On their own sites, businesses must ensure the content they develop is interesting, persuasive and credible, so people want to read and share it. For some businesses, like those working in controversial areas that come in for regular criticism from NGOs, such content might include a film about the part of the world where it operates, or a simple but tough rebuttal document, or a revealing and candid interview with a senior executive. The business could generate thought-provoking content about the future of energy policy that might be genuinely interesting for specialists.

At this point, we need a reality check. Most firms, particularly where they are engaging on important policy issues, will never create content that is going to light up the masses. That is not credible. We are talking about creating content that can at least credibly appeal to the overwhelming majority of people that have any interest in a given policy issue, and hopefully to a significant proportion of the public that take an interest in public debate or, to use a slightly dated phrase, current affairs.

Heathrow Airport's website is a good place to look for high-quality content. It has a great deal of useful material that develops its public case to maintain its position as a hub airport. Simple, short videos and presentations explain why airport hubs are important and how they benefit countries' economies. This material could easily be understood by anyone with a passing interest in the issues, although additional detail is available for those particularly interested. You could imagine all such material being shared through social media.[106]

Content marketing firms are springing up in places like New York to help clients do this in a more thoughtful, systematic way. These firms create content for clients – and often platforms for that content to sit on – which is designed to be read or watched and therefore to shape the opinion of target audiences. The best firms provide an extremely useful service for their clients, one which is going to be in greater demand as the need to influence the public conversation grows.[107]

These same principles apply to the content generated on other platforms. People will not subscribe to a boring Twitter feed and will not *like* – let alone regularly interact with – a Facebook page that reads as if it is an extension of a business' hyper-corporate homepage. People will, however, do so with accounts that push out fun, interesting or unusual material, whether it is specifically on issues relating to the business or not.

Whatever approach a firm takes, content really matters. Whether businesses decide to generate relatively high-brow material designed to appeal to specialists, or light but fun material to be shared and liked on Facebook, they must constantly ask themselves whether they could imagine someone coming across the information, reading it and passing it along to others. If not, then it is not worth developing in the first place.

Mark Wallace at Conservative Home stresses the need to create great content:

> "Online communications demands transparency, speed and personality. Businesses can't just hope to hide dirty secrets, sit on queries for hours or days and respond in robotic corporate language. If you stay silent, give half answers or blather then the story will move on without you on other people's terms.

> "That means companies should provide content up front, make it interesting and go out of their way to share it. No-one is saying you need to be on every social network – it would be lunacy for a City law firm to run a Bebo profile, for example – but if your audience is in a particular space, you need to be there to help set the tone of the discussion. If you don't, the discussion about you will happen anyway but you'll have no way of correcting untruths or addressing complaints."[108]

COMMUNICATE ON DIFFERENT FRONTS

Temperamentally, directors of communications and public affairs for businesses like to give campaigns focus. Rather than chasing media coverage wherever they can get it, they prefer a smaller number of high-impact activities. The thinking is, in this way, while they might get coverage only reasonably regularly, the quality of coverage in content and space is likely to be better.

When conversations on a business mostly took place in the national media, such an approach made sense. Yet the growth of the web has changed the game because of the scale of coverage on a firm – not just through specialist websites and blogs but on social media too. There are simply more conversations taking place. These days, businesses need to take the sort of approach that political campaigns fighting an election take. That means engaging in debate wherever it takes place and seeking to influence debate across multiple platforms to influence the general opinions people form.

The most comprehensive guide to the options businesses have as they start forming their communications plans is provided by David Meerman Scott in *The New Rules of Marketing and PR*. In it, Meerman Scott talks about blogs, podcasts, web videos, email lists, Twitter, Facebook and many other forms of communications that businesses have available to them. Online conversation can take place anywhere, so businesses should be open to using all of these options.

Global brewer SABMiller uses interesting ideas to maximise its communications across different channels. Its homepage is attractive, well laid out and makes a number of strong arguments on key issues affecting its business without appearing too self-obsessed.[109] The website links to an active Twitter feed, a YouTube page (which has some interesting videos), a Facebook page and a LinkedIn page. In addition, there are blogs and detailed materials on its corporate priorities. Wherever they *can* communicate online, they do so.

As a major brewer with significant interests in the developing world, SABMiller inevitably finds itself involved in sensitive debates. Rather than hiding away, or creating material so inoffensive as to be meaningless, SABMiller chooses to engage energetically but thoughtfully in public conversation.

Is there a risk of over-exposure online and being too thinly spread? No. People that work in communications teams of major business find themselves in an unusual position. They see all the material their team develops and it is easy to get the wrong impression about the scale. Most people, including most journalists and "stakeholders", see only a fraction of the material put out online. Businesses should feel relaxed about generating serious amounts of content across different platforms and repeating themselves endlessly.

DEAL WITH UNFAIR CRITICISM

Anyone with even the most limited experience of the web knows the style of communication online is informal, abrupt and aggressive. Bloggers have a different style to news reporters and columnists, and on social media platforms the style of communication is closer to fast-paced conversation, only less polite.

In such an environment, businesses should feel confident in engaging in this informal style and be willing to rebut unfair criticism immediately and unambiguously. False accusations spread fast on the web and where accusations are false people expect to see them corrected. Businesses cannot worry that rebutting will only draw more attention to a story, or the act of rebuttal will make them look aggressive. The rules and conventions of the web are different.

If a well-respected individual comes out and criticises an organisation publicly, a straight, aggressive response can be out of place. However, I have always believed it possible to disagree with anyone publicly if the tone is right – people watching the exchange will always tolerate polite disagreement.

Furthermore, there are many organisations and individuals who at first look formidable but who struggle to deal with any push back.

Many trade unions and NGOs fall into this category – they are great at attack and poor at defence. Pointing out their factual mistakes makes life difficult for them.

Fundamentally, people do not like to be seen to be wrong. While there will always be some who will argue regardless of facts, most people back down. Even if they end up arguing their words have been misinterpreted, people hate being publicly found out.

In his classic book *Hardball*, Chris Matthews writes: "Some of the most memorable campaigns in history have been won by the victims of slanders. In each case, what swept the election was the successful counterattack, the cleverness in calling 'foul'."[110] This is exactly right. While unfair attacks are infuriating, sometimes they provide an opportunity to take the moral high ground – we have seen how important this is – and to question the attacker's motives.

DEVELOP A VOICE OF AUTHENTICITY

Communication on the web – and especially social media – is intensely personal. It sees ordinary people openly sharing opinions on the most sensitive issues without a second thought. This trend for more personal communications is also visible in the mainstream media, particularly on the various newspapers' websites, where journalists are developing more personal profile than ever before.

Businesses cannot engage in this new climate hiding behind corporate formality and anonymity. While it might still be acceptable to provide a comment from a spokeswoman for the *Wall Street Journal*, it is hard for that same anonymous spokeswoman to push back effectively on popular news sites and blogs, and impossible to do so on social media platforms like Facebook and Twitter.

Businesses must cultivate personality online so people are dealing with people and opinion is matched with opinion. A simple first step – and some firms like the Co-Operative in Britain are already touching on this – is giving their Twitter feed an obvious real-world author, even just giving a first name or set of initials.

The same can de done easily on other social media platforms like Facebook. You can already see in the Co-Operative's case that people are more likely not only to deal with individuals, but to engage with them reasonably. People will say all sorts of things to an anonymous corporate account, yet all but the most impolite will think twice before being rude to a friendly, named human being.

Veteran Democrat consultant Joe Trippi, who, as campaign manager for Senator Howard Dean's presidential campaign in 2004 was at the vanguard of online political campaigning, summed this up nicely in *The Revolution Will Not Be Televised*:

> "The internet is not the place for safe, vetted corporate communication. We're not morons. When we get an email from the president of the company, we know it wasn't actually written by him. People would rather get a real email from a real guy in the real mailroom than a phony one from the CEO (who we know is vacationing on his yacht anyway). Sacrifice some of the slickness of your website for the real, sometimes messy quality of the best blogs."[111]

Big businesses should go one step further and develop known and respected public experts as spokespeople. By that I mean they should use some of their communications staff in public much more than they do now – people who can become, with the chief executive, the public face of the business online and elsewhere. Ideally, businesses should also create personalities who are recognised experts in their field rather than just professional communicators who can be seen as paid help.

Given the nature of such roles, it might be that businesses need to change their hiring plans in future. If they are going to develop spokespeople with visible and active public roles, certain attributes will become more important than ever. Spokespeople are going to have to be very confident in the public eye and on camera, quick on their feet, have an attractive personality and ideally an interesting personal backstory. In other words, they are going to require the same skills as many political candidates and their spokespeople.

WORRY ABOUT VISUALS

As we saw in the chapter on emotion, people process messages best of all if they are delivered audiovisually. The combination of seeing powerful imagery and hearing a persuasive narrative makes people feel something and influences their views.

While developing web technology means not everyone can stream everything they want to on their phones and computers all the time, we should assume this is a temporary phenomenon. The bigger challenge is making interesting audiovisual material people want to watch in the first place. Generally, given the ease with which short audiovisual clips can be created, it is worth doing so regularly. If you can put up a film of a spokesperson talking about an issue, it is worth doing. However, it takes serious thought, time and investment in equipment to generate high-quality material.

McDonald's recently made a simple, well-produced and effective corporate video. Responding to a question from a customer about the ingredients for the sauce in a Big Mac, the firm put out a video of their executive chef cooking one of the burgers from scratch in a home kitchen. The video showed the chef mixing together a sauce and then cooking and assembling the burger.

The video was effective in two ways. Firstly, it gave a human face to a big corporation that, while extremely popular, has been relatively quiet in public debate in some parts of the world. Secondly, it made clear that the burger was made up of good, real ingredients. In a world where more people are taking an interest in food and the cooking experience – and organic ingredients – it was a useful piece of positioning. It had clocked up more than 2.5 million views by the spring of 2013.[112]

This might seem like a small benefit for such effort. It is not. A business is never going to produce a single piece of video, no matter how interesting, that will significantly improve perceptions of it in one go. Realistically, reputation management, even if pursued aggressively, is a long process – people can be expected to see business' materials only occasionally and views must therefore be shaped over time. Businesses must keep coming up with ideas that gradually push their image and reputation in the right direction. For McDonald's this short video was a win.

When engaging with the general public, businesses have to be honest about what people will be interested in and what they will sit and watch for a few minutes. They need to ensure it is engaging, visually attractive and fast moving.

MOBILISE PEOPLE WHEREVER POSSIBLE

We know the web creates networks – fleeting and permanent – and these can cause major problems for businesses. It is worth re-emphasising they offer great opportunities for businesses too. Many firms have the potential to mobilise large numbers of people behind them on important issues and they just need the confidence to try.

Mobilising businesses in public conversation is, technically speaking, relatively easy. Social media and access to cheap web technology that helps businesses store data and send email gives every business the chance to create influential campaigns. The thing that stands in the way is nervousness from senior executives over the prospect of unleashing the masses on their behalf.

I have already discussed this area in some detail. The keys to effective mobilisation are the following:

1. Extensive opinion research to enable businesses to create simple messages for people to rally behind and to understand which people will be most likely to join.

2. Creating social media platforms and, above all, a simple campaign site to encourage people to join up to engage in a simple act, like emailing a regulator.

3. Online coverage and a targeted web ad campaign to drive more people to the site.

4. Additional coverage in the mainstream media to highlight support and encourage more people to join.

Such campaigns are labour intensive, but they are one of the few things that businesses can do to turn a public debate on its head. Being able to demonstrate public support can transform how a business, or its position on an important issue, is viewed by outside audiences.

David Wilson at the British Beer & Pub Association, says:

> "In putting digital megaphones in the hands of the public the policy environment has been affected. Businesses need to mobilise the megaphones in their favour. Our beer tax campaign has been a good example of this. We needed to demonstrate that the vast majority of the public had reached their limits of tolerance of tax rises on beer. In the past opinion polls would have been the only tools in the box. Now digital platforms can be deployed to unleash public opinion on politicians craving legitimacy for their actions."[113]

CHAPTER NINE
SHAPING REPUTATION IN THE MEDIA

THE CHANGING ROLE OF THE MODERN MEDIA

THE GROWTH OF public opinion online is becoming the most serious external challenge businesses face – one that should increasingly dominate the thinking of communications teams and senior executives. As the public voice becomes dominant, the media has inevitably become less important in relative terms. However, in this chaotic world, businesses are finding that they are dealing more with the media than before, even as its impact becomes less important.

Many firms are finding that they are answering more calls from the media and are finding their way into more stories. Businesses that want to prioritise the public conversation taking place by focusing resources on the web will still have to find time to deal with journalists writing about them. This is another reason why a clear strategy and a rapid decision-taking process are important – staff need to be able to work quickly and efficiently in this new world.

The growth of the web has brought huge challenges to the media and changed the way they operate. Falling sales and declining ad revenues mean there are fewer journalists on staff in newspapers. In turn, to maintain market share against blogs and other news sites, and to increase online ad revenues, these journalists have to write more copy to fill up space on their publication's websites.

As American PR consultant Ryan Holiday explains in *Trust Me, I'm Lying,* the economics of news sites and the blogosphere in this new world is such that journalists, commentators and bloggers must drive readers to their articles for click-throughs that generate new adverts on new pages and that ultimately create revenue for the sites.[114]

The increased pressure on journalists to create new material means they are turning more to high-impact stories that can be written quickly – stories that emphasise things like gaffes, rows and hypocrisy. Businesses, like political campaigns, therefore often find themselves dealing with endless mini-crises that would previously never have seen the light of day. Speeches or interviews where senior executives admit weaknesses in their businesses are turned into major stories, while minor incidents of poor public service are presented as real brand crises.

The changes in the media over the last 15 years have thrown up new challenges to businesses. As a result they must change the way they approach media relations. In this chapter, I set out those principles businesses need to be most aware of in this new world, while re-emphasising a few others that remain as true today as they were before.

CREATE NEWS OR FACE THE CONSEQUENCES

Before I began working with the media, I naïvely assumed journalists researched their own big stories and secured quotes by making endless calls. I soon realised a huge proportion of stories are manufactured by campaign groups, NGOs, businesses, political parties and an array of other interested parties on behalf of journalists. The new demands on time-strapped journalists for endless fresh content have only accelerated this trend. Outsiders have more opportunities than before to generate news.

If an outside organisation can provide interesting and well-researched stories to a journalist, the chances are they will get written up. This is useful for organisations that can provide a regular stream of ideas, but very damaging for those organisations that struggle to generate material at a time when opposition groups are doing so.

Like political campaigns, businesses must break into from-scratch story generation – and on an industrial scale. Communications teams must prioritise these stories and incentivise staff to create them. Businesses must ensure they always have a few concrete stories ready to go in a given week.

What counts as an interesting story? New product launches, high-profile staff hires, new consumer trends a business has noticed, responses to external events and news stories, insider strategy stories, announcements around expansion, exports to developing economies because of the growth of their middle class, old products coming back, generational or gender differences in buying, surveys and polls, interesting pictures, innovation on social media. This is just a small sample.

In generating such stories, four things count:

1. The communications team carves out time for structured brain storming, rather than just hoping people come up with ideas.

2. At all costs, the team avoids the sort of eye-rolling, cynical culture where people feel inhibited from making suggestions.

3. The communications team talks to journalists all the time and knows them well enough to suggest stories and understand their interests.

4. The communications team is sufficiently plugged in to the technical teams and executive management to get a steady stream of information.

As ever in communications, content counts.

PROVIDE MORE COLOUR

Creating ideas for news stories is crucial for any modern communications team. However, there is an additional demand they must acknowledge in order to get the media to take up their stories with enthusiasm – this is the need to provide what journalists call *colour*.

Anyone that has spent significant time dealing with the mainstream media recently knows journalists increasingly want endless background detail for stories. While the trend towards a focus on personalities in journalism is a long-standing one in politics and elsewhere, there is an increasing focus on the story behind the story.

In politics, this manifests itself as a desire for *process* stories – stories about relationships between ministers, developing policy thinking and so on. Financial news is some way behind but catching up. Think of how the media covers the response of businesses to crises, for example, where a big part of the news story is how the firm has handled the news story itself.

The media's obsession with colour will not change and businesses must respond. They need to get into the same mindset as campaign spokespeople, giving away more details on strategy, how decisions are taken, and on things like the style and leadership of senior executives behind closed doors.

The same approach needs to be taken when senior executives are interviewed. Chief executives should be prepared to talk about their corporate philosophy, how their upbringing and education affected them, who their personal and professional role models are, and about past mentors. Again, journalists will add personal colour and anecdote to their stories whatever happens, so businesses should provide them on their own terms.

For many businesses, this will be hard. Few, if any, chief executives went into the corporate world to become public figures and many find personal conversations uncomfortable; there are some corporate cultures that frown upon apparent profile building. However, whether it is mainly down to the growth of the web, or some other factors, the trend towards more personal stories and the *real* story is here to stay. Businesses need to adapt.

BE CREATIVE IN DRIVING THE MESSAGE

It is becoming more difficult to drive a consistent message to the public because of the fracturing of the public conversation with the growth of the web. However, the dispersed nature of public conversation makes it even more important that businesses try to drive a clear message through the media – a place where large numbers of people will see the same thing.

Contrary to what those of us that work in communications would wish, journalists are never interested in principle in running any organisation's message in its news stories. A firm might want to get across the message their business is all about quality – and they might stress this in the communications around a new product launch. Journalists might prefer to write about the price of the product or about something mundane like its colour. Businesses, like political campaigns, must think hard about how they get their messages to run through their general communications, regardless of what journalists may want to write.

In politics, one way campaigns seek to drive their message through the media is explicitly briefing journalists on their strategy. While it can seem odd to brief strategy in such a way – in that some believe the power of a strategy depends on it being hidden – the reality is campaigns find journalists more likely to amplify their messages if they have been told explicitly what they are and how they play into wider strategy. Journalists are obsessed with process stories anyway, so will often frame stories within the context of strategy, real or imagined. Businesses can get into the same game, being more explicit about their general operational and communications strategies.

A firm that wanted to develop the message that it was obsessed about quality might decide to brief a piece that said its strategy for the next year was in an acquisition drive to take on the best businesses in a particular field. Or it might brief a piece on how it was changing its recruitment and compensation systems to attract and retain the best staff, or that it was seeking to improve staff skills by widening access to paid courses at respected universities.

Businesses should also think about events and moments that allow them to project their messages in a powerful way, without having to rely on journalists reproducing long quotes from their executives in their story (journalists think this is boring).

For example, our business obsessed with quality might develop a story on how it was investing large sums in a new office complex to improve its research and development capability, or that it had upped starting salaries for the best graduates. There are times when this is easier than others, but businesses, like campaigns, can always find more ways to drive home a particular point.

WORRY ABOUT TODAY, NOT TOMORROW

In the 1990s and early 2000s, it became common for those working in media relations in politics to talk about the *news cycle*. Better communications operatives understood when and where to place stories to maximise coverage and influence the public agenda. They understood how to use a mix of morning daily newspapers (in London, out in the late evening before), the evening newspapers (out at lunchtimes), the broadcast news bulletins (throughout the day) and the analysis shows (in the late evenings and at weekends) to play off each other and create an echo effect.

While communications staff can still use different media outlets across different channels to secure more and better coverage, the concept of the news cycle has been completely changed by the growth of the web. In the past, major announcements could be made in the middle of the afternoon so the early evening news bulletins covered the story but it was still fresh enough to be featured in the next day's newspapers.

Now, any public announcements are covered on the web immediately and for the hours that follow. Not only does the online media report stories instantly, but the sort of commentary and analysis that might previously have been expected a day later now comes within the hour. All of this reporting and analysis is seen by vast numbers of people in real time.

What is true in politics is true in the corporate world too. Everyone now has access to news and commentary instantly in a way that was previously only true for those that had access to major news wires like Reuters or Bloomberg. The websites of the quality daily newspapers feature extensive coverage of financial stories, and other online sources that deal with corporate and economic news have proliferated.

Like political campaigns, businesses need to forget old ideas about the news cycle and develop announcement plans assuming instant coverage and near-instant analysis and commentary. That means immediately providing all media with the sort of useful context and background behind major announcements that might previously have been held back for more analytical journalists. It also means having other interesting angles for the media to go out within hours, to ensure that analytical commentary goes in the right direction.

Crucially, businesses also need to broaden their views on who counts as the media. They need to get stories out to a much wider set of people – bloggers, influential people on Twitter and so on – to create as much positive commentary as possible that will not only be seen by more people, but that will also influence those journalists looking to sum up how announcements have been received. Businesses must prioritise good coverage *now*, not tomorrow.

MEDIA OPINION IS NOT PUBLIC OPINION

In politics and the corporate world, people confuse talking to the media with talking to the public, as if the two are the same thing. As newspapers often have a close relationship with their readers and because they increasingly take strong editorial positions on their comment pages and even their news pages, some people imagine they are genuinely representative of public opinion.

This is wrong. While newspapers sometimes accurately reflect the interests of their readers in their choice of news or in their editorial position, they are often miles away from the public on crucial issues. In my experience, most senior journalists have much less insight into public opinion than politicians and campaign consultants, and less in common with the public in their personal views than politicians and consultants.

The growth of web journalism in this more opinionated climate exacerbates this gap. In their need to generate more content, journalists churn out more stories of limited news interest but inject them with a heavy slant designed theoretically to appeal to public curiosity. As discussed above, we seem to see a never-ending tide of stories that emphasise trivial gaffes, attacks and so on. Many of these are totally lost on the public at large.

Communications teams should therefore not necessarily respond to a developing story in a way that the media is taking it. They should not assume the journalist they are dealing with has a window into the public mind – journalists know how to make a story stand out on a page but have no intrinsic sense of whether this will really capture the public imagination. Assuming they are on top of their opinion research and feel confident they know what the public thinks about them and key issues, organisations dragged into the media spotlight should make their own judgements about where public opinion is and where it is heading.

This raises difficult practical questions for those that work in media relations. Communications teams need to ensure that they drive a message primarily designed to reach the public, but they also have to be sensitive to what increasingly opinionated journalists want to write. Businesses that ignore this reality risk being totally marginalised in a story.

According to former Democrat consultant Jon Steinberg, who now works in corporate communications:

> "It means that when thinking about how a story is pitched you have to be much clearer in your mind about what the outlet or reporter is driving their coverage towards to ensure you fit their news agenda. This has been true in politics for years (there's no point in pitching a story about sensible immigration reform to a paper campaigning against immigration) and is increasingly true for business."[115]

The uncomfortable reality is that communications teams need to tread a fine line between satisfying the public and those journalists who will be tapping away at their keyboards on a story.

REMEMBER THE MEDIA'S DIFFERENT AND DIVERGING INTERESTS

It is too often forgotten that the media and communications consultants are in a different game. Their interests frequently overlap, but mostly they do not. On endless occasions, consultants, particularly in politics, develop what look like friendships with journalists, only for those journalists to write a negative story on their candidate or client. Similarly, on endless occasions, journalists spend time cultivating consultants in the hope their relationship will count when a big story emerges, only to find the story has been given to a higher circulation newspaper. The fact is communications consultants and journalists do different jobs and their relationship is transactional.

Consider this comment:

> "[People] should remember the somewhat hyperbolic but
> useful rule made famous by Richard Nixon: The press is
> the enemy. This may seem harsh to some, and so to those
> with gentler ears, let me put the admonition more mildly:
> Always remember what these people do for a living. Their
> mission is to produce a good story, and in their business
> it's generally the bad news that makes the best headlines.
> Failure, misery, disaster – that's what makes the bells go
> off in a journalist's nervous system: the kind of story
> where somebody gets hurt."[116]

This comes from Chris Matthews, a former political aide to senior
Democrat politician Tip O'Neill and now a high-profile political
broadcast journalist. While Matthews was partly joking, the
underlying points he made were serious – journalists have their own
agenda and, while their interests may often overlap with those of the
communications world, this is merely useful. The media use
communications people to help sell newspapers and communications
people use the media to generate coverage for their clients. Clashes
are inevitable.

The increased distance from many in the media to public opinion as
a result of the growth of the web means communications consultants
must keep a degree of psychological distance from journalists. They
have to force themselves to remember at all times their job is to
promote and protect their firm and that public audiences are their
primary target.

FOCUS ON TV

Finally, it is worth stressing a very traditional principle: like political
campaigns, businesses should be obsessed with projecting their image
better through TV. Arguably the best operation at this over the last
few decades was President Reagan's communications team, led by

long-term aide Michael Deaver. Some of the visuals created for Reagan were extraordinary, like his speeches in Berlin where he called on Soviet President Gorbachev to "tear down this wall", or in Normandy on the 40th anniversary of the D-Day landings.

No business is going to have Reagan's command of the news agenda (which allowed him to force broadcasters to run perfect background shots). But with careful thought, businesses can seriously improve their visuals. The first step is being completely clear about the image you want to project. This should, of course, tie in to the general message your organisation is pushing.

If the image the firm is trying to project is about customer service, then businesses should find a way to ensure that executives are pictured with people. If the image to be projected is competence – for example, during a turnaround – the business should find a way of showing executives directing staff and taking decisions.

Some of this can sound a little corny – some of it is – but too many organisations devolve decisions over crucial images to TV producers. Even well-funded political operations – partly to save time, partly because of a lack of confidence – are happy to ask broadcasters to come on a visit and let them dictate what politicians or key speakers do in front of the cameras. When busy, confident and difficult TV producers start dictating backdrops and activities for people they are going to film, it can be hard to stand in their way.

Sometimes this works acceptably well, but at other times TV producers can have a certain shot in mind which might fit in with lazy stereotyping but which does nothing for the organisation in question. If campaigns or businesses do not have a firm view on what image they would like to project, and therefore no firm view on how visuals should work, they will be at the mercy of the broadcasters.

Not every corporate communications team will have people who are experienced with visual imagery, but a great deal can be achieved with a clear view on what message the business wants to project and what images would work best to deliver that message.

CHAPTER TEN
SHAPING REPUTATION IN A CRISIS

HOW CRISES BECAME ORDINARY

THE DIRECT EXPOSURE of businesses to raw public opinion means they are plunged into endless crises. Greater scrutiny, more media coverage, endless public comment and rapidly growing networks all combine to create a hugely challenging climate for businesses. In the past, most were forced to deal with crises only when something very serious happened, like the need for a product recall, a major accident, or particularly ill-advised comments from a senior executive. Now crises for businesses are a regular occurrence.

Not every bad story online marks a crisis of reputation. In their excellent book, *Damage Control*, crisis communications consultants Eric Dezenhall and John Weber rightly argue businesses must keep things in proportion – recognising the difference between a nuisance on one end of the spectrum and a "marketplace assault" on the other.[117]

The problem is that even apparently trivial stories can blow up into real problems because of the web and therefore the combination of greater scrutiny and rapid spreading of information and opinion across networks. Mere nuisances can develop into marketplace assaults. SUBWAY's "footlong" problem, discussed earlier, is an obvious example.

Businesses need to develop skills of public persuasion so they can protect and promote their reputation and image generally. However, they also need to sharpen their skills in crisis communications for when they find that the ongoing conversation about their firm takes a more aggressive turn. They need to work out how to fight more effectively.

Over the last 15 years, I have worked on a number of very high-profile political and corporate crises. Some, if not the majority, have come about because of organisational missteps, while others have come about through unpredictable events. A small number have come from hostile external action. Regardless of the source, the same principles for dealing with crises keep coming up. I explore them in this final chapter.

COMMUNICATIONS IS CRISIS MANAGEMENT

Communications have always been important in a crisis, particularly with the growth of 24-hour news. However, the proliferation of opinion and the media's obsession with the story behind the story means senior executives must prioritise communications in a crisis. The intricacies of crisis management were once interesting only to professionals who did it for a living – and it seemed to be a subject discussed only after the crisis had come and gone.

Now the question over whether a story is being handled right is part of the real-time news story. It is now perfectly possible for a business to deal with a crisis perfectly in the real world but to be criticised in the media because the PR was handled badly. It has become impossible to separate perception from reality – they are the same thing.

While businesses should always focus communications efforts on the public and not let the media force them down a communications route they do not want to take, businesses need to think of the media as a key audience. They need to imagine they are putting on a performance for journalists. If the handling of the crisis looks and feels competent to the media, it will be reported as such.

In a chapter in *Damage Control* titled "Write Your Own Case History", Dezenhall and Weber put it like this:

> "Every crisis manager faces two challenges: managing the crisis and looking good in the process. Does the 'looking good' part sound a bit superficial? It shouldn't. Conveying an impression of competent damage control isn't about pretense or ego. It is an absolutely crucial act of survival. Companies that act effectively behind closed doors but leave it to others to judge their efforts risk being portrayed as inept, arrogant, or worse. Sometimes simply 'doing the right thing' is enough; at other times, gaining recognition for your crisis management labors must be a central part of your response."[118]

Businesses should remember, when events are moving quickly and when details are murky, it is impossible for people to know whether things are being handled correctly or not. When you are in a crisis situation in an organisation, the chances are that you do not even know yourself whether things are being handled in the right way in the real world. You can follow processes and stay focused on the big things, but it takes time to know whether things are being resolved. For the media, things are even less clear – they therefore rely to an even greater extent on *perception*.

WORKING OUT WHAT A CRISIS IS ABOUT

Crises rarely end up being about what you initially think they are. When a crisis strikes, the organisation's first reaction is to collate the facts, deal with the specific problem in the real world and communicate to the media how the problem is being resolved. While the organisation is busily dealing with the specifics of the issue, the real challenge to the organisation's reputation can emerge in a separate place in a more serious way.

For example, imagine reports that a senior executive has wasted a big sum of company money on a lavish holiday with his wife. The initial crisis appears to be a narrow one – a crisis around the behaviour of an apparently out-of-control executive. The response might be to discipline the executive – make him pay back the money and apologise. At this point, the firm might think that the job has been done.

Amid all the focus on the behaviour of this executive, it is possible the real crisis lies elsewhere. The big thing the media and public might be learning from this episode could have been that senior management had lost touch with blue-collar customers, or there was no oversight of senior management from the board, or the business had a problem with honesty. Each is a more serious crisis than one executive blowing money on a holiday.

Businesses must think hard at the outset about the essence of the challenge. Is it really about the incident in question or something more fundamental? When a newspaper's website covers the story about the staff of a bank branch routinely being rude to the public, what is it that will irritate people and what do they want the business do? Maybe it shows the bank views customers as cash cows, or maybe it amplifies problems the bank has got with poor call centres or with its branch closure system.

Businesses have to deal with the specifics of the crisis but the approach they take and the language they use must deal with the heart of the problem. If the crisis is serious enough and damage has been caused to the fundamental building blocks of the brand, it might be the business has to take responsive action outside the specific crisis. Assuming the firm has suffered damage to its reputation for customer service in the crisis, it may be worth creating stories highlighting amazing acts of customer service that staff members have been responsible for, or finding a way to reward the most loyal customers.

The chances are the real challenge will become visible quickly. A good business will know their relative strengths and weakness and have a sense of where the story is going from the earliest conversation. Sometimes, however, the real challenge takes time to emerge. Businesses need to do all they can – monitoring comments from the public under news stories, for example, and by internal conversation – to see where their focus should be.

DEVELOPING AN EMOTIONAL RESPONSE

The explosion of opinion online means crises are rarely about things like poor quality products and increasingly about ordinary people being harmed by a corporate decision or how customers have been mistreated. Crises are invariably presented emotionally and personally. These stories have the potential to be very damaging, for the same reasons we saw in our earlier section on the power of emotional messaging.

People are more likely to pay attention to a crisis and remember it if they have been moved emotionally. Allegations of bad behaviour, unfairness and dishonesty matter, and businesses must engage on this emotional and personal level where appropriate. Businesses generally know this, but I am constantly surprised by the statements senior executives put out during crises – statements that read as if drafted by lawyers that have never met an ordinary person.

There are times when businesses need to protect themselves from future legal action by, for example, not accepting publicly liability for a problem, and times when they will want to avoid encouraging additional claims. However, there is never an excuse for not having communications professionals make the language used in statements more sympathetic to the public mind.

For businesses, an emotional and personal response will often simply mean showing they care about those affected. This is relatively straightforward. If the crisis involves someone being treated badly, they need to imagine it is one of their family members that has been mistreated and take personal action from there.

Sometimes, perhaps often, businesses will have done nothing wrong and be embroiled in a crisis unfairly. In such circumstances, apologies are not required or appropriate. Instead, firms need to fight back robustly to disprove and discredit claims made against them. In all this, the same principles apply – businesses must ensure that their push back is emotional and, where relevant, personal in response.

That does not mean that businesses should go on the attack viciously – they need to retain their dignity and remember their responses will be written up by a journalist they have no control over. They also need to ensure their behaviour and comments reflect their stated values. Businesses should seek to connect with the public in how they position their rebuttal and in the language they use.

If they have been wrongly accused of appalling customer service, businesses need to say something about how they love their customers and appreciate their loyalty, that it goes to the heart of their corporate philosophy and that they were not guilty of what they were accused of. Obvious perhaps, but many businesses rebut false accusations like they were reading events recorded in a police log book.

There is an important caveat to all this. While businesses should apologise where necessary, push back where possible and generally seek to connect with audiences on an emotional level, in crises businesses should seek to do all they can to maintain a reputation for competence. Firms that lose their reputation for competence lose the ability to control the story and they are at the mercy of the media and external commentators. Furthermore, businesses perceived to be incompetent will struggle to deal with the next crisis that comes along. Businesses that mishandle a single story can quickly become, in the eyes of the media, "embattled" or "flailing" the next time around.

Clearly, there is a trade-off here. In exerting firm control – and communicating it – businesses can look hard-edged. The next three issues explain how businesses can maintain a sense of competence, even while developing an emotional response.

CREATE A STEADY INFORMATION FLOW

In a crisis there is always tension between the businesses affected and the media. The firms want to present their case in their own way to protect their reputation; the media is desperate for any news it can report, which is easier if the news is bad for the businesses.

Since it is mainly the journalists covering the crisis that decide whether the crisis is being handled correctly, executives have to provide a steady stream of information. Starving the media of information will irritate them and make it more likely they will write that businesses do not know what is going on, or quote endless numbers of those theoretically affected complaining businesses are not telling them anything (the media's way of saying they are not being told anything).

Consultants Michael Regester and Judy Larkin put it like this in their book on crisis communications: "It is usually when the media believe the organization at the centre of the crisis is unduly slow in providing information, reticent about providing 'talking heads' for interview or thought to be withholding information, that they become hostile."[119]

In complex, fast-moving stories, competent journalists can always get hold of *some* information. There is always someone in organisations, in the middle of a high-profile story, who will leak information. Sometimes this is down to vanity, sometimes miscommunication, sometimes because that person thought it would help. Either way, some information always gets out.

Businesses have to put measures in place to ensure a steady and controlled flow of information. Controlling the information flow does not mean restricting it completely. Rather, it means, as far as possible, getting information out at regular intervals where it can be given an explanation and useful context. This involves the following:

- Ensuring the media know exactly who they can call at any point.
- Announcing in advance that regular briefings will be held at set times to manage expectations.

- Providing reasonably regular access to the senior management for interview.

- Feeding background information to journalists between the briefing times.

In my experience, regardless of whether things work out exactly along these lines, putting in these informal rules with the media has the benefit of looking open, rather than closed, collaborative, rather than obstructive, and organised, rather than chaotic. It also means that briefings given outside of the official ones can be used to develop useful background narratives and to drop in useful colour.

On occasion, this approach might feel like more of an aspiration than a real plan, but businesses should do all they can to keep some sort of control.

KEEP UP A SENSE OF MOMENTUM

There are two shared characteristics between the media and public that make crisis communications difficult. The first is they want to see visible progress quickly. The second, which is related, is they have completely unrealistic expectations about how long it takes to sort out even apparently minor problems. These two issues make *momentum* in a crisis particularly important for businesses.

By momentum I mean the *sense* that decisions are being taken to move firms forward in a crisis. Momentum allows businesses to guide the media and public through the journey of a problem arising to its being dealt with. Crucially, it allows resolution to be achieved through the mere visible presentation of a path to resolution.

Momentum in a crisis can be developed in the following way: firstly, businesses are seen to establish the full facts and to take immediate steps to stabilise the problem (stopping things getting worse); secondly, businesses are seen to deal with specific problems created; thirdly, businesses establish a clear explanation for why the crisis occurred; fourthly, businesses are seen to take steps to ensure such a problem can never happen again; finally, businesses are seen to be compensating those affected.

The fourth part is particularly important in drawing a line under the crisis and is a key part of showing that the businesses are competent. Sometimes the measures firms say are being taken will be cosmetic but this is less important than being seen to take action. The businesses might put in place new training programmes for staff, or they might bring in new staff, or they might fire people – to some extent, in communications terms in a crisis, being seen to act is everything. This is what I meant earlier when I said momentum allows businesses to demonstrate resolution by showing a path forward – businesses do not necessarily need to have, for example, trained everybody in new ways of working, or introduced new checking procedures. Rather they need to use momentum to show that things are well underway.

This might all sound like a statement of the obvious – these steps are surely those that any vaguely competent businesses would follow? In themselves, that is true, but businesses can sometimes forget that crises have a natural life cycle of interest for the media and publicly visible action must take this into account. Senior executives cannot unilaterally decide when a crisis is over – it has to be played out.

Some crises will come and go in a few hours, while more serious ones will have a longer cycle. Either way, the same cycle should often be followed to use momentum as a positive force. Businesses need to keep this cycle in mind as they seek to manage the coverage on their crisis. There is no point, for example, trying to close down a massive crisis to your reputation simply by saying that steps have been taken to ensure it could never happen again if people do not know what happened and why.

EFFECTIVE DECISION-TAKING

As we have seen elsewhere, decision-taking is treated seriously by campaigns – corporate communications teams need to learn how to create a culture that has a bias for action. This is even more important in a crisis. These days, even apparently simple crises with few moving parts can rapidly escalate because the web and social media are able to play in endless new comment very quickly. By the time firms react the story is established and a full-blown crisis has emerged.

In a crisis businesses must ensure they have the ability to take decisions fast. Ideally, they will have the fundamentals of this in place already – the communications team will already operate at a rapid place and have an understanding with the chief executive and the board that allows them to take decisions regarding communications without the need for endless checking. But, while a crisis is sometimes purely related to reputation, often it is a real-world logistical or operations crisis.

Maybe new products are found to be unsafe, or maybe businesses have suffered an accident. BP's Gulf of Mexico is the most extreme example I can think of in recent times which was a genuinely massive operational crisis. In such circumstances, clearly businesses need to establish dedicated teams – teams that are likely to include the chief executive and representatives from the communications, legal and operations departments. That team must be capable of taking decisions in one meeting – which must be repeated regularly.

If there is a dedicated crisis team that then ends up having to have further meetings with the most senior staff, or experts on the ground, then decisions will not only be slow but they are unlikely to be the right decisions. Tactical decision-taking on the ground is, of course, the responsibility of local decision-takers, but big decisions must be taken by one team in one room.

DO WHAT YOU CAN TO PREPARE

The final issue to consider is the importance of preparation. While every crisis is different, businesses can prepare for crises in general. Firstly, most obviously, businesses can ensure there is a dedicated crisis team, that everyone on it knows they are on it and who else is on it, that everyone knows where they should report to in a crisis and that everyone has everyone else's contact details. Speaking from experience, it is shocking the number of times people are scratching around for people's mobile numbers late at night when they should be communicating a response.

All businesses should create a general crisis manual that explains this in more detail, including details of which members of staff are responsible for which functions. For example, from a communications perspective, the director of communications should know who is responsible for updating the website outside office hours, who is going to be taking calls from the media on a given day and so on.

Related to this, businesses can also run crisis simulation exercises on likely crises that may occur. These will vary in scale and sophistication, depending on the type of operation. For example, clearly a corporation that runs nuclear power stations is going to require a vastly more serious crisis preparation operation than a business that sells financial services products. But the rise of opinion means that all businesses can face crises regularly and all businesses can and should prepare.

Logistical preparation is vital – and relatively straightforward with careful thought – as is the experience that comes from crisis simulation. However, businesses should also do all they can to prepare staff to think for themselves – to be flexible, adaptable and decisive.

Crises can often be averted or resolved more quickly than they otherwise might be if staff can use their initiative to take the right action at the earliest opportunity. Communications teams should spend time regularly running their own tactical decision games that test their staff's responses to mini crises. An Advanced Course on Communications – a sketch of which can be seen in the Appendix – will also help substantially.

CONCLUSION
INTEGRATED COMMUNICATIONS

CORPORATE COMMUNICATIONS TRANSFORMED

FOR A HUNDRED years, corporate communications has been dominated by elites that considered the public as a passive mass to be manipulated. Communications professionals cared what people thought, but they did not care what people said. The views of the public were irrelevant because they could not be heard.

Even a decade ago, communications teams worried far more about what small numbers of influential journalists said than vast numbers of ordinary people. This inevitably produced a world that was introspective and that emphasised the sophisticated metropolitan values taken seriously by the media and other elites that ran the communications industry.

The sudden and recent arrival of the public voice – of democracy – in shaping the image and reputation of modern businesses is a genuine revolution. It has completely changed the nature of the communications challenge. An entire industry has been exposed to a set of challenges that had never existed.

Those businesses and agencies that think the rise of the web and social media requires only slight changes to their working habits, and that their focus on elites should continue, not only miss the point, but are working in an industry that will soon become sidelined. The reputations of modern businesses are no longer primarily shaped by elites in the media and "stakeholders", but by the public.

In this new world, it will be the natural tendency for some communications teams to reach for simple, bolt-on solutions that will help them deal with the new challenges they face and exploit new opportunities that arise. Inevitably, many will turn to web specialists that can help them develop better websites and create attractive social media platforms.

Technical expertise is helpful, but secondary. As I have argued throughout, businesses must put *people* first – and remember that their web platforms are purely a means to an end. Instead of impressing highly educated, metropolitan elites whose job it is to think and write about the world, they now have to engage with and appeal to ordinary people whose role in public conversation is a small sideshow to their everyday lives.

THE IMPLICATIONS OF CHANGE

The corporate advertising and marketing industries can claim they have always kept the public in mind. Professionals in this environment have been more concerned about public opinion because they have taken opinion research and metrics more seriously. But their skills – important as they are – have still been deployed from 30,000 feet. They have never been forced into public conversation.

It is this public conversation that businesses must now prioritise. They must focus on what people are saying on social media platforms, blogs, specialist web forums and in the comments section of relevant newspapers. This does not mean that they should ignore the mainstream media, which is still hugely influential (especially for the biggest companies), but that they should be realistic about where the bulk of commentary is coming from and where customers and potential customers are going to be most influenced.

The most successful businesses in leading public conversation will have a very clear idea about what they want to achieve. They will have a strong sense for the overall communications approach they want to take, a specific plan to bring this approach to life and they will take decisions quickly. They will know who to influence and how to reach them. Crucially, they will have a general sense for how they should deal with their key audiences and specific knowledge on how to move them on key issues – strategy combined with operational competence.

I believe getting to this position requires businesses to follow the same approach to communications as political campaigns. Political campaigns are, after all, accustomed to robust, two-way public dialogue. They are used to shaping the image of their candidates on issues that matter in a giant public conversation. For them, the development of the web and social media changes the tactics, but not the fundamentals of what they do.

Campaigns have demonstrated success by focusing on the set of fundamental skills I have outlined in this book:

1. Embracing a scientific approach that values testing, targeting and metrics.

2. Creating language that moves people on an emotional level.

3. Mobilisation of trusted third parties in the form of endorsements.

4. Organisational design to facilitate rapid decision-taking.

5. Creation of effective strategy.

Competent tactical implementation flows from these skills.

Some businesses may argue that it is naïve to encourage greater focus on such fundamental issues or to argue for a more public-centric approach. They will argue that this is exactly what they are doing already. My response would be this: across the businesses I have worked with I have not seen it regularly or effectively. In my experience, very few firms have genuinely accepted the nature of the challenge created by the explosion of online opinion. Few businesses are truly configured to deal with public debate.

For example, while many businesses spend time and money on testing and targeting for their advertising and marketing campaigns, relatively few engage in public debate using this same approach. Similarly, few businesses think sufficiently hard about how to move opinion through their public messaging. Some businesses focus on endorsements, but on nothing like the scale that political campaigns do. On corporate strategy and decision-taking, there is competence at both the executive and operational level, but less in communications. Here, strategy and organisational design are seriously discussed only rarely.

Perhaps the best evidence of this lack of acceptance is the fact that many businesses still run their communications on the old tripartite model. Typically, this model clearly separates advertising and marketing – normally the senior partner – from media relations and public affairs. Very often, these teams sit in their own silos, occasionally even in different offices.

The scale, style and pace of public conversation around modern businesses strains this tripartite model beyond breaking point. When the web and social media mean that your business is being discussed publicly by huge numbers of people, it no longer makes sense to have separate teams working in separate silos.

THE FUTURE OF CORPORATE COMMUNICATIONS

The huge increase of opinion that we have witnessed in recent years is no flash in the pan. The role of the public in shaping the image and reputation of modern businesses is going to become even more pronounced as the old models of communications – radio, TV, newspapers and even traditional, informational websites – are replaced by platforms that encourage the airing and sharing of opinions.

There is no possibility people are going to go back to sitting and listening to the reporting and commentary of elites. There is an irreversible trend towards public engagement – people want to engage with friends, with those that share similar interests, and also with those who will simply respond back and make life interesting. Facebook and Twitter may be around forever, or they may be replaced in the public's affections with other platforms; but people will still talk.

Given this, the tripartite model is redundant. The future of effective corporate communications is in the creation of integrated, extremely flexible teams that can respond very quickly to the changing public debate around their firms, and can shape that public debate in the way they wish.

Such an approach demands that the advertising and marketing teams, the media relations teams, and the public affairs teams, act in concert to promote a particular image for businesses and to protect them where challenged. They must do this using whatever channels they can to affect public opinion. Such an approach also demands businesses start to recruit different skills – people who are expert in dealing directly with the public, rather than people who have been used to transmitting messages one-way to the public.

Businesses should strongly consider following the political world by integrating their communications teams under the equivalent of a campaign manager (most likely a director of communications) – someone whose job it is to have a view on the overall reputation and image of the business, rather than one part of it. Working in a war room environment, senior staff with different responsibilities and skills would come together to form, shape, and protect the reputation and image of businesses.

These changes should be mirrored in the agency world. While it makes sense for some agencies to specialise in particular areas, it also makes sense for others to become specialists in public opinion more generally by offering a broader set of services to help businesses with the challenges they face.

If businesses move away from the tripartite structure, they will increasingly expect their agencies to help them communicate generally. PR and public affairs agencies should therefore take steps to move into advertising and marketing, for example, but particularly to move into all things digital.

Regardless of how it unfolds specifically, businesses and agencies must reconfigure and put the management of public opinion first.

A WORLD OF OPPORTUNITY

There is no denying the arrival of democracy in the corporate communications world has brought serious challenges to huge numbers of businesses, and particularly those that are high-profile and public-facing. Many businesses now face much greater scrutiny and endless public commentary. Getting to grips with this new world is hard.

This new world also offers the most extraordinary opportunities for those that show enthusiasm for public debate. The networks that can cause pain for businesses can also be used to spread positive messages. The online campaigns that are mobilised to put pressure on businesses can be mobilised in the opposite direction. Powerful movements can be created to change the way people think about key issues. Firms that could not get a reasonable hearing by elites in government and in the media on issues that matter to them can now *force* people to listen to them.

In short, the best businesses will thrive on this new chaos. They will be helped by greater public exposure because their products are popular, their customer service is good, and they actually *like and respect* ordinary people. The best firms will realise that democracy is here to stay and they should therefore get ahead of the game.

APPENDIX
AN ADVANCED COURSE IN COMMUNICATIONS

WHY WE NEED AN ADVANCED COURSE

WITH A FEW exceptions, the corporate communications and public affairs industries have never taken staff development sufficiently seriously. While many businesses and agencies offer induction courses for new staff and rotation schemes designed to develop graduates, businesses and agencies do not routinely teach advanced skills in communications, or more general skills in decision-taking and strategy. Junior staff are expected to learn on the job – under senior staff supervision – and senior staff are expected to be the finished article.

Fundamentally, this is a reflection of the lack of interest in innovation in much of the communications world. Some firms *are* breaking into areas like grassroots mobilisation, web video production, app development and detailed opinion research. But many, if not most, firms in these industries still operate as if we are in the 1990s, when reputation management was all about formal press releases, elite dinners and general mass advertising.

Whether this is a cause or effect of much of the communications world's lack of interest in innovation, many people, even at the most senior levels, take little interest in developments in relevant fields like cognitive research or psychology, and do not follow cutting edge innovation in political campaigns. Where ideas about innovation do

Meet the People | James Frayne

spread, it is often because columnists in the mainstream media feature them in their articles – and it still takes a significant amount of time for these ideas to be taken up seriously.

This is all a problem for two reasons. Firstly, it is a problem because of the explosion of opinion. The mass exposure of businesses to public opinion means agencies and businesses must focus on developing those skills designed to influence public opinion. These skills are difficult to master and unlike those the corporate communications and public affairs worlds have, for the most part, been focused on in recent times. Without these skills, businesses will struggle to manage their reputations.

Secondly, it is a problem because many staff fail to reach their full potential, or take long periods of time to do so. Some staff learn quickly, either because of obvious natural talent, because they have been exposed to a challenging period that extended their experience, or because they have been lucky enough to work with a talented mentor. But many in the communications world go through long periods where they learn little and talented staff destined for senior positions find it difficult to take the next step up because they have not accumulated necessary skills and experience.

No one working in communications can claim to be the finished article and everyone has more to learn, but there seems to be a particular gap in the market for teaching the middle-to-senior ranking staff described above – people who have perhaps been working in the industry for six or seven years and who are desperate to take a leap into leadership roles. These are intelligent people, who show management potential, but who might not have had the chance to develop certain crucial communications skills in their roles to date.

Many universities do offer courses in communications – some even offer part-time courses for more experienced practitioners – but these tend to pass over fundamental skills such as organisational design and decision-taking. Most focus on important but more tactical skills, such as improving writing and presentation.

The teaching of specific skills and exposing staff to best practice and new developments in the communication industry would be extremely useful in principle. Many staff would benefit from knowing, for example, the basics of recent developments in cognitive research. However, the objective of the course would be to improve the ability of staff in *how* to think and *how* to approach problems. It would be a course designed to produce future leaders that can come up with creative ideas to help their clients or their firms.

For these reasons, while much of the course would be taught, there would need to be regular exercises designed to get staff thinking about and taking their own decisions. Many staff – even those who have been operating at relatively senior levels for some time – take truly independent decisions irregularly and rely on more senior staff for the really big decisions like strategy creation and message development. Regular war gaming sessions and tactical decision games (TDGs) would help to develop these crucial skills.

A SKETCH CURRICULUM

I set out below a sketch curriculum for how the Advanced Course in Communications would operate. Inevitably, it reflects my own beliefs on what is important in communications and therefore much of the content of this book. The skills outlined here are general, but some agencies and businesses would demand an approach tailored to their own needs. Some, for example, might want a greater emphasis on crisis communications, while others might want to focus more on the art of persuasion.

EXERCISE ONE: A BRIEF HISTORY OF THE COMMUNICATIONS INDUSTRY

- The growth of the mass media
- The rise of advertising and public relations
- The rise of TV and the golden age of mass communication
- The development of modern public affairs
- How the internet changed everything
- Profiles of some of the greatest communicators

EXERCISE TWO: THE COMMUNICATIONS INDUSTRY TODAY

- An overview of the various strands of the wider communications industry
- About the rise of opinion and the growth of public opinion power
- The profile and role of the modern mainstream media
- An exploration of the blogosphere and online news

EXERCISE THREE: STRUCTURE, DECISION-TAKING AND MANAGEMENT

- The challenges facing organisations in affecting opinion
- The principles of effective decision-taking
- Why the war room concept works
- How to create decentralised management systems
- An examination of how the best communications operations are structured
- Creating the right team
- The principles of effective management
- TDGs to explore effective decision-taking in action

EXERCISE FOUR: STRATEGY AND MESSAGE DEVELOPMENT

- An explanation of what strategy is and its importance
- How to create strategy
- Case studies of effective strategy making
- The principles of effective messaging
- How to create effective messages
- Running war games to create strategy
- Running mock messaging sessions to create messaging for theoretical businesses

EXERCISE FIVE: INFLUENCE AND PERSUASION

- How the mind works and the fundamentals of cognitive research
- A history of developments in science, psychology and social sciences relating to persuasion
- The role of emotion in decision-taking
- The power of TV and advertising – the importance of visuals in communications
- Case studies of the use of influence and persuasion in communications and social policy

EXERCISE SIX: OPINION RESEARCH, MICRO TARGETING AND METRICS

- The importance of opinion research
- The modern research industry
- How to develop micro targeting operations
- Case studies of successful micro targeting operations
- The importance of metrics
- Designing the right metrics for an organisation
- The interplay between research, targeting and metrics
- Sessions to design research programmes, targeting operations and metrics

EXERCISE SEVEN: CRISIS COMMUNICATIONS

- The principles of effective crisis communications
- Case studies of success and failure in crisis communications
- TDGs to run through crisis communications scenarios

EXERCISE EIGHT: TACTICAL ENGAGEMENT ONLINE

- The principles of effective online engagement
- An overview of modern tools and websites to help implement successful campaigns
- Case studies of recent successful online campaigns
- TDGs to practice online engagement

EXERCISE NINE: TACTICAL ENGAGEMENT IN THE MEDIA

- Likely future developments in the media
- The principles of effective media engagement
- Case studies of successful media campaigns
- TDGs to practice media engagement

EXERCISE TEN: INTEGRATED CAMPAIGNS: LESSONS FROM CAMPAIGNING

- How political campaigns work
- Case studies of past campaigns
- The benefits of integration
- How businesses can use integrated campaigns

REFERENCES

INTRODUCTION

[1] E. Bernays, *Propaganda* (Ig Publishing, 2005), p.47.

CHAPTER ONE: THE RISE OF PEOPLE POWER

[2] www.nypost.com/p/news/local/this_hero_is_coming_up_short_RzxQNoGFTSdY0AeooGxBiP

[3] articles.latimes.com/2013/jan/25/business/la-fi-mo-subway-footlong-20130125

[4] www.marketingweek.co.uk/opinion/whisky-into-water-is-no-fix-for-too-many-customers/4005913.article

[5] media.ofcom.org.uk/facts

[6] pewinternet.org/Static-Pages/Trend-Data-(Adults)/Internet-Adoption.aspx

[7] pewinternet.org/Commentary/2012/March/Pew-Internet-Social-Networking-full-detail.aspx

[8] pewinternet.org/Static-Pages/Trend-Data-(Adults)/Online-Activites-Total.aspx

[9] www.nielsen.com/us/en/newswire/2012/consumer-trust-in-online-social-and-mobile-advertising-grows.html

[10] Comments made to the author.

[11] Comments made to the author.

CHAPTER TWO: HOW BUSINESS RESEMBLES POLITICS

[12] **news.blogs.cnn.com/2012/07/27/how-the-chick-fil-a-same-sex-marriage-controversy-has-evolved**

CHAPTER THREE: TESTING AND TARGETING

[13] Comments made to the author.

[14] Comments made to the author.

[15] This polling operation is described in detail in Dick Morris' *Behind the Oval Office: Getting Reelected Against All Odds* (Renaissance Books, 1999) and in Douglas Schoen's *The Power of the Vote* (Harper Collins, 2007), pp.211-249.

[16] Comments made to the author.

[17] Schoen, *Power of the Vote*, p.234.

[18] Morris, *Oval Office*, p.207.

[19] Comments made to the author.

[20] Comments made to the author.

[21] 'Why Obama Is Better at Getting Out the Vote', **Slate.com** (5 November 2012).

[22] L. Wunderman, *Being Direct: Making Advertising Pay* (Random House, 1999).

[23] Comments made to the author.

[24] Comments made to the author.

[25] Comments made to the author.

[26] D. Kerpen, *Likeable Social Media: How to Delight Your Customers, Create an Irresistible Brand, and Be Generally Amazing on Facebook* (McGraw-Hill, 2011), p.25.

[27] Kerpen, *Likeable Social Media*, p.27.

[28] M. Lewis, *Moneyball: The Art of Winning an Unfair Game* (W.W. Norton & Company, 2004).

[29] K. Rove, *Courage and Consequence: My Life as a Conservative in the Fight* (Threshold Editions, 2010), p.366.

[30] M. Halperin & J. F. Harris, *The Way to Win: Taking the White House in 2008* (Random House, 2006), p.277.

[31] S. Issenberg, *The Victory Lab: The Secret Science of Winning Campaigns* (Crown Publishers, 2012), p.263.

CHAPTER FOUR: MESSAGES THAT MOVE PEOPLE

[32] S. Koch, *Double Lives: Stalin, Willi Munzenberg and the Seduction of the Intellectuals* (Enigma Books, 2004), p.15.

[33] S. McMeekin, *The Red Millionaire* (Yale University Press, 2004), pp.103-122.

[34] Koch, *Double Lives*, p.37.

[35] W. Lippmann, *Public Opinion* (Harcourt, Brace and Company, 1922), p.205.

[36] You can view all the main Presidential campaign ads at The Living Room Candidate (**www.livingroomcandidate.org**).

[37] Available at The Living Room Candidate (**www.livingroomcandidate.org**).

[38] G. Le Bon, *The Crowd: Study of the Popular Mind* (Classic Books International, 2009).

[39] R. Cialdini, *Influence: The Psychology of Persuasion* (Harper Business, 2007).

[40] T. Schwartz, *The Responsive Chord* (Doubleday, 1974), p.84.

[41] S. Pinker, *How the Mind Works* (Penguin, 1999).

[42] D. Westen, *The Political Brain: The Role Of Emotion In Deciding The Fate Of The Nation* (Public Affairs, 2008), p.16.

[43] D. P. Redlawsk et al, 'Affective Intelligence and Voting: Information Processing and Learning in a Campaign', in R. W. Neuman (ed.) et al., *The Affect Effect: Dynamics of Emotion in Political Thinking and Behavior* (University of Chicago Press, 2007), p.153.

[44] D. Kahneman, *Thinking, Fast and Slow* (Allen Lane, 2011).

[45] T. Brader, *Campaigning for Hearts and Minds: How Emotional Appeals in Political Ads Work* (University of Chicago Press, 2006), pp.131-139.

[46] Graber, D., *Processing Politics: Learning from Television in the Internet Age* (University of Chicago Press, 2001), pp.35-36.

[47] Brader, *Campaigning for Hearts and Minds*, pp.162-163.

[48] Reagan's speeches can be viewed at the website of the Ronald Reagan Presidential Foundation and Library (**www.reaganfoundation.org**).

[49] In 2003, the *New York Times* had an interesting feature on President George W. Bush's visual media operation (**www.nytimes.com/2003/05/16/us/keepers-of-bush-image-lift-stagecraft-to-new-heights.html**).

[50] S. Popkin, *The Reasoning Voter: Communication and Persuasion in Presidential Campaigns* (University of Chicago Press, 1994), p.43.

[51] Graber, *Processing Politics*, p.37.

[52] F. Luntz, *Words that Work: It's Not What You Say, It's What People Hear* (Hyperion Books, 2007), p.184.

[53] P. E. Tetlock, *Expert Political Judgment: How Good Is It? How Can We Know?* (Princeton University Press, 2006).

[54] D. Green and A. Gerber, *Get Out The Vote: How to Increase Voter Turnout* (Brookings Institution, 2008).

[55] Issenberg, *The Victory Lab*, pp.196-200.

[56] **www.gov.uk/government/news/governments-nudge-unit-goes-global**

[57] Comments made to the author.

[58] **www.bbc.co.uk/news/uk-politics-17851992**

[59] **news.bbc.co.uk/1/hi/education/7815481.stm**

[60] Luntz, *Words that Work*, pp.1-33.

[61] J. Klein, *Politics Lost,* (Doubleday, 2006).

[62] J. Gaylord, *Flying Upside Down* (GOPAC, 1991).

[63] J. Carville and P. Begala, *Buck Up, Suck Up... and Come Back When You Foul Up: 12 Winning Secrets from the War Room* (Simon & Schuster, 2003), pp.111-112.

CHAPTER FIVE: GENERATING ENDORSEMENTS

[64] C. Cillizza, *The Gospel According to The Fix: An Insider's Guide to a Less Than Holy World of Politics* (Broadway Books, 2012), pp.95-108.

[65] Comments made to the author.

[66] Comments made to the author.

[67] Comments made to the author.

[68] Comments made to the author.

[69] Edelman Trust Barometer 2012, available on the Edelman website (**trust.edelman.com**).

[70] **www.harpers.co.uk/misc/content/article/5756-wsta-launches-responsible-drinkers-alliance.html**

[71] **news.bbc.co.uk/1/hi/england/london/7259368.stm**

[72] **www.campaignforhsr.com**

[73] **www.terminatetherate.org**

[74] **news.bbc.co.uk/1/hi/uk/7740700.stm**

[75] **nycbeveragechoices.com**

[76] **thehill.com/business-a-lobbying/199245-k-streets-top-10-lobbying-victories-of-2011**

[77] **en.wikipedia.org/wiki/Working_Families_for_Walmart**

[78] **www.americanenergyworks.org**

CHAPTER SIX: TAKING THE RIGHT DECISIONS

[79] Comments made to the author.

[80] S. Popkin, *The Candidate: What it Takes to Win – and Hold – the White House* (Oxford University Press, 2012), p.100.

[81] A behind the scenes look at the Clinton war room in action can be found in the documentary *War Room*.

[82] Carville and Begala, *Buck Up, Suck Up... and Come Back When You Foul Up*, pp.56-58.

[83] M. Matalin and J. Carville, *All's Fair* (Touchstone, 1995), p.243.

[84] **www.iwm.org.uk/visits/churchill-war-rooms**

[85] Two of the best books on Boyd are Chet Richards' *Certain to Win* (Xlibris, 2004) and Frans Osinga's *Science, Strategy and War: The Strategic Theory of John Boyd* (Routledge, 2007). Boyd's presentations are available online (**dnipogo.org/john-r-boyd**).

[86] J. Santamaria, V. Martino and E. K. Clemons, *The Marine Corps Way: Using Maneuver Warfare To Lead A Winning Organization* (McGraw-Hill, 2004).

[87] Santamaria, Martino, Clemons, *The Marine Corps Way*, pp.91-92.

[88] The Institute for Security and Resilience Studies (**www.ucl.ac.uk/isrs**).

[89] Comments made to the author.

[90] D. Vandergriff, *Raising the Bar* (Center for Defense Information Press, 2006).

CHAPTER SEVEN: CREATING EFFECTIVE STRATEGY

[91] Rumelt, R., *Good Strategy Bad Strategy: The difference and why it matters* (Profile Books, 2011), p.5.

[92] Rumelt, *Good Strategy Bad Strategy*, p.2.

[93] Rumelt, *Good Strategy Bad Strategy*, p.7.

[94] Comments made to the author.

[95] The BBC had a good summary of the campaign just before the end (**news.bbc.co.uk/1/hi/uk_politics/3968183.stm**).

[96] *Wall Street Journal*, 7 November 2012.

[97] Rove, *Courage and Consequence*, pp.363-364.

[98] Rove, *Courage and Consequence*, p.388.

[99] Popkin, *The Candidate*, p.35.

[100] P. Schwartz, *The Art of the Long View: Planning for the Future in an Uncertain World* (John Wiley & Sons, 1998), pp.134-162.

[101] Comments made to the author.

CHAPTER EIGHT: SHAPING REPUTATION ONLINE

[102] Comments made to the author.

[103] Comments made to the author.

[104] **www.bp.com**

[105] David Meerman Scott has a very good section on the need for businesses to generate interesting content in *The New Rules of Marketing and PR: How to Use Social Media, Online Video, Mobile Applications, Blogs, News Releases, and Viral Marketing to Reach Buyers Directly* (John Wiley & Sons, 2011).

[106] **hub.heathrowairport.com**

[107] For example, see this Business Insider article: (**www.businessinsider.com/why-ge-target-and-credit-suisse-are-creating-content-2012-11**).

[108] Comments made to the author.

[109] **www.sabmiller.com**

[110] C. Matthews, *Hardball: How Politics is Played, Told by One Who Knows the Game* (Free Press, 1988), p.125.

[111] J. Trippi, *The Revolution Will Not Be Televised: Democracy, the Internet and the Overthrow of Everything* (Harper Collins, 2004), p.215.

[112] You can watch the video on YouTube (**www.youtube.com/watch?v=rcu4Bj3xEyl**).

[113] For more information on the British Beer and Pub Association's campaigns, visit their website (**www.beerandpub.com**).

CHAPTER NINE: SHAPING REPUTATION IN THE MEDIA

[114] R. Holiday, *Trust Me, I'm Lying* (Penguin, 2012).

[115] Comments made to the author.

[116] Matthews, *Hardball*, p.183.

CHAPTER TEN: SHAPING REPUTATION IN A CRISIS

[117] "Marketplace Assault" is a term used by crisis communications consultants Eric Dezenhall and John Weber in their book *Damage Control: Why Everything You Know About Crisis Management is Wrong* (Portfolio, 2007), p.24.

[118] Dezenhall and Weber, *Damage Control*, p.145.

[119] M. Regester and J. Larkin, *Risk Issues and Crisis Management in Public Relations: A Casebook of Best Practice* (Kogan Page, 2008), p.192.

INDEX

Lightning Source UK Ltd.
Milton Keynes UK
UKHW020603270619
345140UK00005B/227/P